The Grand River

The Grand River

DUNDALK TO LAKE ERIE

WOOD ENGRAVINGS

by Gerard Brender à Brandis

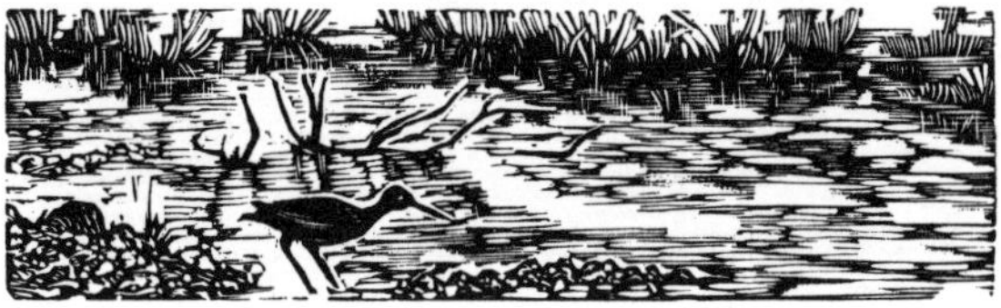

WITH BACKGROUND TEXT

by Marianne Brandis

Marianne Brandis

Gerard Brender à Brandis

The Porcupine's Quill

Library and Archives Canada Cataloguing in Publication

Brender à Brandis, G., 1942–, artist

The Grand River : Dundalk to Lake Erie / wood engravings by Gerard Brender à Brandis ; with background text by Marianne Brandis.

ISBN 978-0-88984-381-3 (paperback)

1. Grand River (Ont.)—History. 2. Grand River (Ont.)—In art. 3. Brender à Brandis, G., 1942–. I. Brandis, Marianne, 1938–, author II. Title.

FC3095.G72B73 2015 971.3'4 C2015-901798-X

2 3 4 • 17 16 15

Published by The Porcupine's Quill, 68 Main Street, PO Box 160, Erin, Ontario NOB 1TO. http://porcupinesquill.ca

Edited by Chandra Wohleber. Represented in Canada by Canadian Manda. Trade orders are available from University of Toronto Press.

We acknowledge the support of the Ontario Arts Council and the Canada Council for the Arts. The financial support of the Government of Canada through the Canada Book Fund is also gratefully acknowledged.

Canada Council for the Arts
Conseil des Arts du Canada
Canadä
ONTARIO ARTS COUNCIL
CONSEIL DES ARTS DE L'ONTARIO
an Ontario government agency
un organisme du gouvernement de l'Ontario
Ontario
Ontario Media Development Corporation

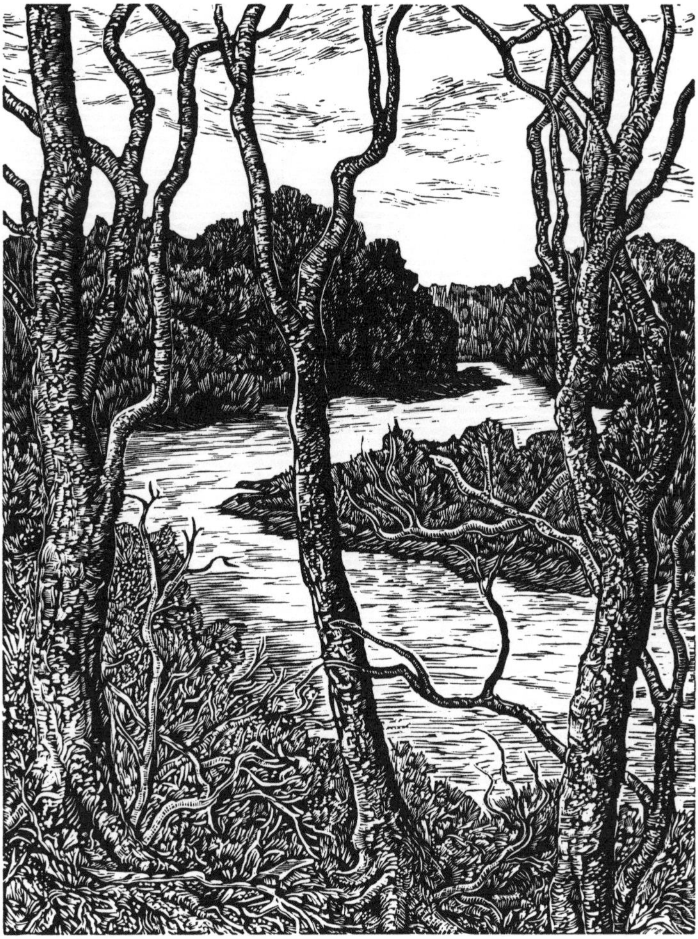

— *Introduction: Living with a River* —

An artist is sitting on the bank of a river, drawing in a sketchbook. He's perched on a shooting stick; its tip, half-buried in the gravel, is only a few inches from the edge of the gently rippling water. Beside him on the ground lies a battered tin box, open, holding pencils, a pencil sharpener, an eraser.

The artist is Gerard Brender à Brandis; it is his wood engravings that you'll see in this book. I'm a few yards away, sitting on a slope where the earth is padded with dry leaves and grass and twigs. Propped against my knees is a notebook. I look, listen, reflect, write. I record details of the scene in front of us. I listen for birds. I observe how water flows and how land and water meet. I think about water, I feel the air, I watch the clouds. Here are all four of the medieval elements—earth, air, fire (the sun), and water—of which, in that ancient but by no means irrelevant conception, everything else was composed.

The river that we're observing is the Grand, in southwestern Ontario, but the story that this book tells is also, by analogy, the story of many others because rivers the world over have much in common. This river valley is a microcosm of the biosphere and of the planet: the history of this river is that of the evolution of a landscape, of human settlement, of development and exploitation, of damage and reconstruction. A similar story can be told of many parts of the planet's land surface, because that surface is a jigsaw puzzle of watersheds. Each of us lives in one. Every gutter along a city street, every culvert under a country road, every weed-filled ditch beside a farm field, every ravine and canyon, reminds us that we live in a watershed. Each watershed is three-dimensional—surface, underground, and air; it, and the environment that it holds in the palm of its hand, are created and sustained by rivers.

As well as being the river's biography in space and time, this book is about how two artists perceive the river and have come to understand its importance to the part of the planet that it flows through. In images and words we reflect on 'riverness', the private life of rivers, the dialogue between land and water, the connections with vegetation and climate and weather, with humans and their works.

The story of the river and the watershed is a human story, a very Canadian one, about First Peoples, explorers, immigrants, and what they brought and created here.

This river—here—is everywhere.

— *Riverness* —

Rivers are a crucial part of the life of the planet. They are vital to the climate, indispensable to the amount and quality of water, essential for the removal of waste. They make and unmake agriculture and the food supply.

At the core of every river's life story is water and its interaction with land. There is a constant dialogue. Moving water created the river's valley and channel, and it continues to shape them. The water we see interacts with the water below the surface that we don't see and that, through vegetation, transpires into the air to help create weather and climate, vegetation, habitat for animals and humans, the entire ecosystem. All the water in the valley is connected in one way or another with the river and its tributaries, and every drop goes through several uses and incarnations on its way from source to mouth.

In all the settled parts of the planet, the dialogue is really a conversation—often an argument—among land and water and humans. Settlement affected the river, and the river both co-operated and retaliated.

— *Geography and history* —

The Grand River runs for nearly three hundred kilometres through southern Ontario, emptying into Lake Erie. The river that we see now dates from the period when the last glaciers were melting, about 12,000 years ago, but beneath it is an older river system that existed before the last glaciation and ran in a more west-to-east direction to Lake Ontario. Even the present river originally flowed into Lake Ontario.

As the last ice sheets retreated, the exposed land acquired vegetation and wildlife and, before long, people came. The first Paleo-Indians, who arrived about 11,000 years ago, were hunters of the woolly mammoths, mastodon, elk, caribou, and grizzly that then lived in the area, but by about AD 900 their successors were beginning to settle and grow corn. They established villages, which they moved as the soil in each place became depleted. Archaeologists have uncovered hundreds of sites along the Grand, particularly the lower section, where there are signs of early occupation by First Peoples.

European contact was at first indirect. Trading among First Peoples brought European goods inland stage by stage from the Atlantic coast and the St. Lawrence before the peoples of what is now southern Ontario actually met Europeans. Among the first to reach the area were missionaries; the Récollet missionary Joseph de la Roche Daillon and two French traders visited the Hamilton-Brantford area in 1626–27. Fur traders came; the Native residents quickly learned that furs were valuable.

The peoples then living here were Huron and Attiwandaron (Neutral), both Iroquoian. In 1640–41, the Jesuits Jean de Brébeuf and Joseph-Marie Chaumonot came across a large fortified Attiwandaron village near Brantford and spent the winter there. François Dollier de Casson and René Bréhant de Galinée—Sulpician missionaries and explorers—spent the winter of 1669–70 probably at or near the mouth of the Grand.

In the middle of the seventeenth century, during a war resulting from alliances between the First Peoples and the Europeans, and the desire to control the fur-rich region, the Iroquois (the Six Nations) from the Finger Lakes area in what is now upper New York State defeated and scattered the Hurons and Neutrals. The victorious Iroquois did not create many permanent settlements—their homeland was still around the Finger Lakes—but they used the region north of Lakes Erie and Ontario for hunting and trapping and established some bases for those activities. War and disease had weakened them, however, and in the mid-1690s an Ojibwa people, the Anishinabe or Mississaugas, moved southwards into the area, waging war with the Iroquois and defeating them.

Nearly a century later, it was from the Mississaugas that the British government purchased extensive tracts of land in southwestern Ontario. This included the Grand River valley, which General Sir Frederick Haldimand, the governor of Quebec (which then included present-day Ontario), bought in 1784 as a new home for the Six Nations who, as a result of fighting alongside the British during the American War of Independence (1775–1783), had lost their lands in New York State. So it was that the Iroquois—Haudenosaunee, the People of the Longhouse—came back to the Grand River region, this time to settle.

The grant, according to the wording of the original document, consisted of a strip of land ten kilometres wide on each side of the Grand River from its source to its mouth. The Six Nations' leader, Joseph Brant, negotiated the arrangement.

The Six Nations—Mohawk, Cayuga, Onondaga, Oneida, Seneca, and Tuscarora—arrived in the Grand River valley in that same year. With them came small numbers of Delawares, Tutelas, and others. Each nation created one or more villages, scattered along the river from present-day Brantford to Lake Erie. When the Six Nations Reserve was created, many of them moved there. In 1847 Mississaugas from the Credit River settled on a small adjoining reserve.

In the early days, the Mohawk Village was the main settlement, reflecting the fact that the majority of the migrants were Mohawks. The village was in the southern part of what is now Brantford, at a ford across the river that had perhaps been used for millennia.

A few miles from the Mohawk settlement was Davisville, a village created by Thomas Davis, a Mohawk chief and cousin of Joseph Brant's. Davis was a fervent Methodist and his village, which for a few years included Mississaugas as well as Mohawks, was religiously oriented.

The relationship between the Six Nations and the British government—including its colonial representatives in what became Upper Canada in 1791—was a troubled one. Joseph Brant and his people considered that the area of the grant was too small to be a viable hunting territory but too large for them to cultivate, with their limited numbers. Moreover, European settlers were already moving in and clearing land.

At the outset, Brant had given substantial tracts to European friends of the Mohawks who had been neighbours in the Finger Lakes area and had fought alongside them during the war—people like the Nelles, Young, and Dochstader families. A few years later, believing that the Six Nations held the land in freehold, Brant decided to sell some of it to European speculators who would in turn sell it to settlers. The money raised would be put into an annuity for the Six Nations, and Brant hoped that the Iroquois men would learn farming from the European farmers: the Six Nations relied to a considerable extent on agriculture as well as hunting and trapping but it was the women who had always done the farm work. It was obvious to Brant that the hunting and trapping way of life was becoming steadily less viable in the context of private land ownership and increasing deforestation and settlement. The men would, like their European neighbours, have to become farmers.

Brant's transfers of huge blocks to speculators brought him into conflict with the colonial government, which declared that the Six Nations did not have freehold to the land and were not entitled to sell it. In 1841, the Six Nations were established on what is now the reserve south of Brantford.

— *European settlement* —

The accounts of the first European settlers who came to the area after 1784 mention meeting a few trappers who lived in the valley. Other Europeans had travelled through it: during the American War of Independence, Loyalist troops came this way because they helped to defend the British posts along the St. Lawrence and Great Lakes from Montreal to Michilimackinac.

After Brant's transfers to speculators, Europeans came flooding in. United Empire Loyalists arrived, their ranks including people with roots in many different parts of Europe. Mennonites came, looking for more land and for freedom from civic office and military duty. Black settlers arrived—escaped slaves, former slaves freed because they had fought for the British, and still-enslaved Blacks who were brought by their owners and were subsequently freed. Immigrants also came directly from the British Isles and other parts of Europe.

All these groups brought their skills and ambitions, their religions and customs. The imprint remains visible in place names and family names as well as in architectural styles, religious institutions, and cultural traditions: the Germans in Kitchener, the Scots in Galt. Mennonites continue to wear traditional dress and use horse-drawn vehicles and farm equipment.

The influx happened so quickly that by 1793, when the arguments and negotiations were taking place about whether the Six

Nations were entitled to sell the land, so many settlers were already established that moving them would have been no easy matter.

Drawn by the valley's rich resources, all these pioneers cleared land and built churches and blacksmith shops and schools. The river provided power for the gristmills, sawmills, woollen mills and others that are so essential to settlement. Before long, the supplying of local needs expanded into 'industry'. The work of clearing land for farming developed into logging, with timber being floated downriver to sawmills that produced lumber to be sent farther afield. By the middle of the nineteenth century agriculture was also an industry: wheat, flour, and pork were being shipped out.

In the area from Paris downriver, gypsum (plaster of Paris) was mined. Augustus Jones, surveying the land for Lieutenant-Governor John Graves Simcoe in 1793, had noticed outcrops of gypsum, which was an important building material and was also used for fertilizer. The town of Paris derived its name from it. It was often mined by means of horizontal tunnels into the riverbank or a hillside but in other places the location of the beds required vertical and then horizontal shafts. It was either processed locally or sent downriver to gypsum mills in towns like Caledonia. The deposits contained very high-quality gypsum, and mining in the valley continued until the early years of the twenty-first century.

Natural gas was found in Ontario in 1866; in fact, some gypsum deposits were discovered while drilling for natural gas. The lower Grand River valley still contains a fair proportion of the wells in the province.

— *The Grand River Navigation Company* —

Early on, people began to talk about building a canal in the area. Stretches of the lower river were navigable, but between them were rapids and shallows. Before railways and good roads existed, canals were a solution to many transportation problems. This was the era of canal fever; the Industrial Revolution in England was inextricably connected with the building of canals to transport raw materials and finished goods, and in the United States the Erie Canal had been completed in 1825. The Rideau Canal was finished in 1832.

The first serious discussions that involved the Grand River came from William Hamilton Merritt, a Niagara-area businessman, and he was talking about a canal to bypass Niagara Falls—a project that became the Welland Canal. There was repeated talk of using the mouth of the Grand as the southern terminus of the Welland.

The connection between the Grand River and the Welland Canal was more than talk. In 1828, during the building of the first Welland Canal, it was found that at what was called the Deep Cut the instability of the soil caused landslides that made it impossible to dig the Cut deep enough so that it was below the level of Lake Erie. Another source of water was needed—water that could be fed in at a higher level than that of Lake Erie—and so in 1828–29 a canal, the Feeder, was built from the Grand River to join the Welland Canal upstream from the Deep Cut. To raise the water level sufficiently, a dam was built across the Grand at Dunnville. The Feeder, little more than a ditch at first, was immediately enlarged and became a waterway in its own right, allowing shipping to move from the river to Lakes Erie and Ontario. Until 1881 it was an essential source of water for the Welland Canal. In the early 1840s a branch of the Feeder was built from Stromness to Port Maitland so that the Welland had a second western terminus on Lake Erie, below the Dunnville dam; in fact, from 1845 to 1850, during construction of the Second Welland Canal, the mouth of the Grand was the only Lake Erie outlet of the Welland. Along the Feeder, industry developed, including shipbuilding.

Meanwhile, talk continued about the advantages of constructing a canal system along the river, and beginning in 1834 the Grand River Navigation Company built eight locks and six dams, and dug stretches of canal, so that ships could travel along the river as far as Brantford. Towns arose to serve the construction work and were nourished by the water power available at the dams and by the traffic along the river and into the hinterland. Goods were shipped through the canal system. Gypsum, sawn lumber, and agricultural products travelled downstream, while upstream came merchandise to meet the needs of settlers and industry. Steamboats, barges, and scows travelled back and forth; there was a regular passenger service from Brantford to Buffalo.

The Grand River Navigation Company went bankrupt in 1859 but some shipping, such as the transport of gypsum, continued for a time along the river and the Feeder; the latter was occasionally used into the early twentieth century.

Railways came to the Grand River area at about the time when the Grand River Navigation Company closed its books. The first, in the 1850s, were the Great Western and the Grand Trunk; a second burst of railway building took place in the 1870s, and at the end of the century came a number of electric railways, both urban and interurban. All of them transformed the area, facilitating travel and commerce and changing people's thinking about time and geography. They gave a boost to the towns through which they passed and led to the decline of those they missed. Brantford and the Waterloo-Kitchener-Cambridge area were the main beneficiaries but many smaller towns also had rail service—until the railways themselves declined in the later twentieth century.

— *Deterioration of the watershed* —

Settlement and industry had a severe impact on the Grand River watershed. Forests had been cut down to clear land for the farming on which the newcomers' lives depended, and wood was also needed for buildings, fences, fuel, and roads. At its worst point, about the end of the nineteenth century, forest cover in the watershed was down to perhaps 5 or 6 percent. As a result of the clearing, the river's levels fluctuated drastically. Because the soil no longer held the snowmelt and spring rain, the water poured down into the river all at once, taking topsoil with it, flooding towns and washing away bridges and buildings, eroding bottomland and damaging the forest and farmland on it. By the 1930s, floods were an annual event.

Later in the summer, there was drought. Water levels would be so low that riverside towns had insufficient water for residential and industrial needs, and at times the stream consisted of little more than wastewater. Besides sewage, the river also received agricultural effluent, industrial discharge, and many other forms of pollution, such as sawdust from the mills. Because it provided drinking water as well as carrying sewage, low water—indeed, polluted water at any time—was a health hazard.

And of course the summertime drought was a problem for farmers—not a trivial issue because what affects farming affects everyone who eats.

Concerns about the river's welfare and that of the land and people along it began as early as 1880. In that year James Young, writing the history of Galt and Dumfries, made the connection between land-clearing and flooding. In 1905, Kitchener engineer W.H. Breithaupt began calling for government action.

The artist Homer Watson (see p. 84), who lived on the bank of the river in Doon, was one of those who well understood the importance of preserving old forest—and not only because it formed the subject of many of his paintings. He was one of the leaders of a group that bought Cressman's Woods, part of what is now Homer Watson Park, along the bank of the Grand just downstream from Kitchener. In 1913 the woodland came up for auction; learning that it was likely to be bought by the owner of a sawmill, a group of citizens including Watson formed the Waterloo County Grand River Park Co. Ltd., with the artist as its first president, and bought the land. To a meeting of the company Watson reported that the area had been visited by 'Mr Leavitt of New York' (probably C.W. Leavitt, landscape architect, urban planner, and civil engineer), who was familiar with tracts of virgin forest in various parts of the U.S.; he had told Watson that no forest he knew of contained finer trees than Cressman's Woods.

For many years this group carried the responsibility of maintaining the woods. The area is now part of a larger park that comes under the umbrella of the City of Kitchener, Waterloo Region, and the Grand River Conservation Authority.

— *Preservation and remediation* —

It was these water issues—flood, drought, pollution—that led to the realization that the river had to be managed. In 1934 the Grand River Conservation Commission was founded. It was the first watershed management agency in Canada and comprised municipalities along the river. Between 1938 and 1942 it built the Shand Dam, the first dam in Canada to be built for flood control, and planted more than five million trees. Its success led to the Conservation Authorities Act of Ontario in 1946, which resulted in the creation of thirty-six conservation authorities across the province.

In 1948, under this act, the watershed's municipalities formed the Grand Valley Conservation Authority. The GVCA acquired many wetlands, forests, and other natural areas, and also parkland for recreational activities. The two organizations merged in 1966 under the name the Grand River Conservation Authority, a corporate body that still exists today and through which the municipalities of the watershed manage water and other natural resources. It works with governments, universities, and private organizations. It continues to acquire land and to plant trees but its work involves many other watershed issues as well.

Finding solutions to the river's problems is an ongoing task. As a result of vigorous tree planting, the forest cover in the watershed is now up to about 19 percent, and new plantings consist of combinations of native species rather than only evergreens. Water levels in the whole watershed are controlled by seven dams and reservoirs. To filter at least some of the agricultural chemicals from farm runoff, farmers are encouraged to maintain or plant buffer zones of native vegetation along the banks of streams. Fisheries are being protected or rehabilitated. Waste water passes through municipal sewage-treatment plants before returning to the river. To improve the environment and quality of life in the region's cities and to increase the watershed's forest cover, the GRCA pays attention to urban forests—on streets, in parks, and on private property—providing guidelines for choice of species and the ongoing care of trees.

This remediation comes at a time when there are new pressures on the ecosystem. The growing cities in the middle stretch of the river make increasing demands on water supply. Because mining and aggregate extraction threaten the amount and quality of water in aquifers, the actual sources of water are a focus of increasing concern. Cities encroach on farmland just when growing populations need more food. Furthermore, people rightly consider the river a prime resource for recreation—walking, fishing, hunting, canoeing, camping. It's still/again a beautiful river, and preserving or restoring its attractiveness is a worthwhile endeavour.

Two important issues at present are resilience and biodiversity. Putting in place elements that increase the area's resilience will help to deal with the effects of climate change. The pioneers' clearing of forests and draining of wetlands seriously damaged the resilience of the watershed; much of the work of remediation can be described as restoring resilience. Biodiversity—protecting species at risk, and preserving and restoring a variety of ecosystems to provide habitat—improves the environment for us all and protects our life-support system.

In the Grand River watershed there is a wide range of ecosystems and habitats. Among the most important is the Carolinian life zone along the lower stretch of the valley, roughly south of Highways 401 and 402. While covering only about one-quarter of 1 percent of Canada's land area, it contains more species of flora and fauna than any other ecosystem in the country. Its name derives from the fact that it contains many species of trees and other flora and fauna that are found in the Carolinas and reach the northern edge of their range in southwestern Ontario. Although it also includes wetlands, tallgrass prairie, savannah, beaches, and freshwater habitats, it is best known for its forests (where may be found broad-leaved trees such as sugar maple, basswood, hickory, black walnut, and sycamore), of which there are many types in microclimates created by different soil types, moisture conditions, and quirks of natural and human history.

However, this precious ecosystem—found nowhere else in Canada—is also one of the most threatened. Southwestern Ontario is comparatively heavily populated and there are immense pressures on the Carolinian zone. It holds close to one-third of the country's endangered species of plants and animals.

Already at Confederation most of the original Carolinian forest had been cut down. The main surviving remnants are along the Niagara escarpment, on the flood plains of some rivers, and on the reserves: the single largest block is on the Six Nations Reserve, roughly 50 percent of which is wooded.

Many individuals and organizations—principally the Carolinian Canada Coalition—are working to protect what is left of this ecosystem and to restore some of what has disappeared.

All of this makes the Grand a very 'managed' river, but that management and control are easy to forget—and, if you happen to think of it, to forgive or even be grateful for—when you're sitting by the water on a quiet fall day watching a heron fishing and imagining yourself back into the early life of the valley.

— *People, families, society* —

The story of a river always includes the story of the people who have lived along it, who contributed to its life and made it what we see now. Several are dealt with later in this book, in connection with specific locations, but some others also caught my attention and awoke my curiosity.

Joseph Brant (Thayendanegea, 1743–1807) is one of the best known and most important figures in the history of the Grand River. In 1784 he led the Six Nations to this valley to establish a new home on the Haldimand tract. In the following years, he spoke for and represented them in the transfer to European speculators of large parts of this land, and those transfers were a major factor shaping the human settlement of the river.

He had a difficult life. Because the Mohawks of what became New York State were, in Brant's youth, living closely with Europeans, he grew up in a world where contact was common and mostly cordial, though the encroachments of new European migration put pressure on the Six Nations' lands. In this context he had to evolve an identity that combined both Mohawk and European elements, and because of his prominence this was more complex and had more repercussions than was the case for other people.

Brant travelled almost incessantly. In his early and middle years much of this was war-related. In his teens he took part in the Seven Years' War (1756–63) and later he was a war chief and leader in the American War of Independence (1775–83). He seems to have been 'the perfect soldier', energetic, courageous, an excellent leader, and a gentleman. In his later years, a time of comparative peace, he tried to create a confederacy of First Peoples that would link groups in the United States and Upper Canada. He worked to make a home for his people on the Grand. He had to negotiate the very difficult and constantly shifting relations between the British, the First Peoples, and the emerging and land-hungry United States. He travelled to England twice to confer with high government officials. For a man with limited education, and for whom English was a second language, these must have been major challenges; the fact that he achieved what he did suggests much about his character and innate ability.

His first wife, whom he married in 1765, was an Oneida, Neggen Aoghyatonhsera, with whom he had two children. After her death in 1771 he married her half-sister, who died after a short time, and then in 1779 he married Catharine, a clan matron of the matrilineal Mohawks and half-sister of the tribe's leading sachem (chief). They had seven children, and she survived him. Her prominence supported Brant in his leadership of the Six Nations.

The part of his life that concerns us most is his connection with the Grand River. When the land along the river was granted to the Six Nations, he established his family and cleared land for a farm at the Mohawk Village. There also was built in 1785 the Mohawk Chapel—officially Her Majesty's Royal Chapel of the Mohawks, the first Protestant church in Upper Canada and now the oldest surviving church in Ontario. By 1788 the village comprised about four hundred people. Brant's house, the principal building other than the church, was a stopping place for travellers; everyone was made welcome. Life in the Brant home was European; as a host, Joseph was a European gentleman, and Catharine a handsome hostess. They used fine china and silverware and served excellent wines. There were about twenty indoor and outdoor domestics, including Black slaves.

On the first of May, every year during his residence at the

Mohawk Village, Brant presided over a great festival that combined Native traditions with aspects of a European country fair. First Nations people came from miles away and camped by the river.

But Brant's leadership was challenged by some groups among the Six Nations. Because of this hostility, in about 1802 he moved to the head of Lake Ontario, where he died in 1807. The Joseph Brant Museum in Burlington is a replica of the house that he built there.

Augustus Jones (1757/58–1836), the government surveyor, turns up several times in the history of the Grand River. It was he who surveyed the area that Governor Haldimand granted to the Six Nations and he seems later to have surveyed the upper part of the river as well. He surveyed the land which the Mennonites' German Company bought from speculator Richard Beasley. At that time, probably no one knew the whole valley better than he did. He also worked along most of the north shore of Lakes Ontario and Erie and throughout southwestern Ontario, and he surveyed what would become Yonge Street. It was while surveying Dundas Street for Simcoe that he noticed the gypsum beds along the Grand River. He often worked in winter because it was easier to travel and work when the trees were bare, and he was thoroughly at home on snowshoes and in a canoe. He was a close friend of Joseph Brant and in his later years farmed close to the Mohawk Village.

In an Ojibwa ceremony he married Tuhbenahneequay, the daughter of a Mississauga chief, with whom he had at least two sons, one of whom was Peter Jones (Kahkewaquonaby), the Methodist missionary (see below). He was also, at the same time, married to Sarah Tekarihogen, the daughter of a Mohawk chief who was Joseph Brant's brother-in-law, with whom he had eight children.

Peter Jones (1802–56) (Kahkewaquonaby), Augustus Jones's son, had an impressive career as a Methodist minister and chief of the Credit band of the Mississaugas. Because his stepmother, Sarah Tekarihogen, was a prominent Mohawk, he was adopted by the Mohawks and spent seven years of his youth living on the Grand among the Six Nations.

In 1828 Jones was chosen to be a chief of the group of Mississaugas living on the Credit River near York/Toronto. The group had been dwindling and had lost almost all its hunting and fishing grounds; it was obvious that in order to survive they would have to adopt a settled life and learn to farm. Jones did a great deal to promote this, and Methodism was part of his strategy for restoring his people's self-respect. In his youth on the Grand River he had worked with Thomas Davis (see p. 11), the founder of Davisville, and now he took a number of the Credit River group to live in Davisville for a few years.

Like Joseph Brant, he mediated between his people and the Europeans, work that involved his travelling several times to England, where his public speeches attracted large audiences. He journeyed throughout what became Ontario, recognized as a leader of the First Peoples and offering his vision of how they might survive and even play a part in the new world being created around them. In 1847, when the small reserve on the Credit River came under too much pressure from European settlement, he negotiated with the Six Nations of the Grand River and obtained for his people the area in the southwest corner of the reserve that is now the New Credit Reserve.

On his first trip to England he met a young Englishwoman, Eliza Field, also a Methodist, and they were married in 1833. She helped him extensively in all his work. They lived first on the Credit River, then at the Munsee Mission in southwestern Ontario, and finally in Brantford, in a still-existing house called Echo Villa.

The Jones family, like that of the Johnsons and others (see below) shows the intermarriage that was taking place between First Peoples and Europeans. Two of Brant's daughters married Europeans, and a number of White Loyalist men married Six Nations women. This blending of ethnic groups is part of the story of the Grand River valley.

Like Augustus Jones, William Dickson (1769–1846) was also connected with several parts of the Grand River. He was born in Scotland and in 1785 came to Canada, where he prospered as a merchant before becoming engaged in land speculation. He was involved in the Six Nations' land transfers, acting as agent and lawyer (he had been granted a licence to practice). In payment he received about 2,000 hectares of land at the mouth of the river. He also handled the Mennonites' land purchases.

He speculated for his own benefit. In partnership with a cousin, Thomas Clark, he bought one of Joseph Brant's blocks of land where, with his agent Absalom Shade, he established the town of Galt. He actively promoted settlement by Scottish immigrants; John Galt, after whom he named the village on the Grand, was an old school friend of his.

Though undoubtedly a tough businessman, Dickson provided livestock, implements, and provisions to his settlers, advanced money to them, and did not require large down payments.

In 1825 he moved his family from the Niagara Peninsula to Galt, but he returned to Niagara in 1837, leaving his sons to manage the family's businesses on the Grand.

David Boyle (1842–1911) was connected with the river in a very different way. He was born in Scotland and brought by his parents to the Elora area in 1856. He trained as a blacksmith and used that occupation to support himself while he went to grammar school; his aim was to become a teacher, and he obtained his first teaching post in 1865 in Middlebrook, a few miles west of Elora. He was a fine teacher and in 1871 became principal of the Elora Public School.

Already in Scotland he had become interested in archaeology, and during the 1870s he added biology and geology to his list of enthusiasms. He helped to resurrect Elora's then-defunct Mechanics' Institute library and used it to continue his own education. In 1873 he established the Elora School Museum, which by the end of the decade possessed one of the best natural history collections in the province. He also founded the Elora Natural History Society to generate wider public interest in science. His students helped him to look for interesting fossils in the Elora Gorge. Since the publication in 1859 of Darwin's *Origin of Species*, there had been much discussion of evolution and the related issue of the extent of geological time. Boyle was in touch with these ideas but still had one foot in earlier thinking. His book *On the Local Geology of Elora* was published in 1874.

In 1881 he moved to Toronto to work for a publisher of school texts; two years later he gave that up to open a bookshop. He joined the Canadian Institute, a learned society that was laying the foundations for scientific archaeology in Ontario, and became the curator of its museum. He also began a project to make an inventory of all archaeological sites in southern Ontario. In 1887 he sold the bookstore and became Canada's first professional archaeologist. His extensive fieldwork proved to be of lasting importance.

He also engaged in ethnological work. Having established good relations with the Iroquois of the Six Nations reserve on the Grand River, he undertook a study of traditional religious ceremonies there. The result was a very important paper on conservatism among the Iroquois.

No career has only one root, but unquestionably David Boyle's has one of its principal roots in the Elora Gorge on the Grand. What he learned there was a springboard not only for his own life's work but also for the development of archaeology and related disciplines in Canada.

Pauline Johnson (1861–1913) was also profoundly connected with the Grand River. She was born and raised in Chiefswood (see p. 108); her father was George Johnson, a Mohawk chief, and her mother was Emily Howells, a middle-class European woman from a Quaker background. George and Emily met at the parsonage of Emily's brother-in-law Adam Elliott, the missionary who at that time worked among the Six Nations from his base near Middleport on the Grand River. George's father, John 'Smoke' Johnson, had at his christening been given his surname by Sir William Johnson, the Irish-American Indian superintendent and longtime friend of the Mohawks, and Joseph Brant was Smoke Johnson's godfather. Emily raised her four children, of whom Pauline was the youngest, by English standards but never let them forget the importance of their Mohawk heritage. Pauline, therefore, had a foot in each world and that fact was crucial in the career that she shaped for herself.

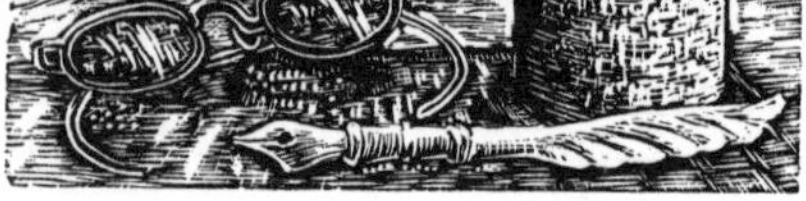

For two years she attended school on the reserve—where she and her siblings did not fit in and were unhappy—and then for two years she went to Brantford Central Collegiate. During that time she was also educating herself by reading in her parents' excellent library at Chiefswood.

After George Johnson's death in 1884, the widow and her two daughters, Evelyn and Pauline, moved to Brantford. Pauline began writing as a way of establishing a career. In 1892 this led to her becoming a public performer; for seventeen years she was touring so constantly that, from her mother's death in 1898 until her own retirement in 1909, she never had an actual home. She worked mostly but not always with a colleague. Altogether she made at least seven tours of western Canada, nine of the Maritimes, four of the American Midwest, and five of the eastern seaboard of the United States, as well as two trips to England. Her financial position was usually perilous, and she suffered from several serious illnesses.

Her divided heritage was reflected in the costume she wore for her performances: she usually wore Native dress for the first half and European ladies' evening wear after the intermission.

She herself wrote everything that she performed: poetry, skits, and a great deal of prose. Much of her work was also published. She proclaimed and celebrated her Native heritage even though she was only three-eighths Mohawk; the Mohawk name that she adopted, Tekahionwake, was actually that of her great-grandfather.

She had a remarkable career. At a time when actors and other public entertainers were distinctly beyond the pale of polite society, she was a welcome guest in the best drawing-rooms. She used her intelligence, creative talents, and charm to make extensive contacts among the powerful, drawing on social connections that often had their origin in the entertaining that the Johnsons did at Chiefswood. She appealed for help to important figures: Clifford Sifton provided some financial assistance, and Sir Wilfrid Laurier wrote letters of introduction. In England she was the protégée of the Canadian-born author Sir Gilbert Parker and of the Canadian financier Donald Smith, who was by then Lord Strathcona, the Canadian High Commissioner.

At the same time she was comfortable with the people she met in prairie villages and in rough mining towns in the Kootenays. She established working partnerships with a series of other entertainers, mostly men, but was always the leader. In a time when travel was uncomfortable and sometimes barely safe she travelled either with her current colleague or alone.

In 1909, already suffering from breast cancer, she retired to Vancouver, continuing to support herself by writing numerous stories and articles for magazines in Canada and the U.S. Interestingly, her doctor at that time was a member of the Nelles family of the Grand River. She died in Vancouver in 1913 and is buried in Stanley Park.

Her travels from coast to coast taught her much about how the First Peoples lived, and the conversations in elegant drawing rooms showed her how they were regarded by Europeans. In her time, the gap between the two groups was widening; she used her work and her public position to try to bridge it.

There are aspects of her life and work that make Pauline Johnson especially interesting today. She claimed a First Nations identity, she used her literary talents to advance a social cause, and she was amazingly popular, but it is more complicated than that. She was both a Native storyteller and an artist working in a European tradition; she was both a middle-class lady and a bohemian free spirit, a New Woman; she was an intellectual as well as a popular entertainer; she was adept at addressing both the elite and the general public. As a Native and an unmarried woman, she occupied the margins of her society, yet she placed herself in the Iroquois tradition of strong women. And, living at a time when a newly confederated Canada was consciously exploring and defining its identity, and regarded the First Peoples as rapidly heading for extinction, she was a vocal defender of the significance of First Peoples in the national mosaic. She was not only the most visible Canadian Native person of her time but also the foremost Canadian woman poet of the period, winning critical recognition and becoming an international celebrity. Interest in her, after slumping during the middle of the twentieth century, is reviving.

In another area of artistic endeavour, the beauty of the Grand River valley inspired painters. The first major one, Homer Watson, will be dealt with later (see p. 84), but there were others.

Carl Ahrens (1862–1936) was born in Winfield, west of Elora, but soon moved with his family to Berlin (now Kitchener). He became a dentist, apprenticing in Stratford and then going to the United States. But he wanted to be an artist and at age twenty-five he moved back to Canada, to Toronto, where he began learning by trial and error. He painted in Waterloo County, becoming especially known as a painter of trees, and in the 1920s he and his second wife settled in Galt, where he attracted friends from politics as well as the arts; William Lyon Mackenzie King was an occasional guest. In his last years Ahrens suffered from many serious health problems. He continued to paint, but his work did not sell well, and he and his wife were penniless. It was Mackenzie King who arranged for Ahrens to live for the last months of his life in the Toronto Psychiatric Hospital.

Lawren Harris (1885–1970) belonged to the Brantford family whose farm-machinery company amalgamated with that of the Masseys to create Massey-Harris. He was a leader in creating the Group of Seven in 1920. He was a fine landscape painter whose work evolved into abstract forms after his move to Vancouver in 1940. Like many other painters, he travelled and painted in a wide geographical area, but he began life on the Grand River.

A.J. Casson (1898–1992) is associated with the Grand River through his work rather than his personal life. He was born in Toronto and spent much of his life there, but during the 1920s he painted regularly in the Elora area. In 1926 he was invited to join the

Group of Seven, having already painted with some of its members during the earlier 1920s.

Carl Schaefer (1903–95) was born in Hanover, west of Waterloo. He studied at the Ontario College of Art, being taught by the Group of Seven's Arthur Lismer and J.E.H. MacDonald. He painted the rolling fields of the Waterloo area. In 1940 he won a Guggenheim Fellowship, and he was an official war artist. After the war he taught at the Ontario College of Art, and from 1952 to 1963 he was an instructor at the Doon School of Fine Arts, established in what had been Homer Watson's home and studio.

— *Overview of the river* —

So far we have not looked at the Grand River as a whole. A journey down it, such as the one that Gerard and I metaphorically made (a short stretch at a time) and—in this book—invite readers to make, takes us through sections that have distinct histories, characters, and moods.

In the upper reaches the river itself is relatively little altered by humans, though much of the land along it has been cleared for agriculture. Here are the basic elements of landscape: water, soil, and vegetation both natural and agricultural.

At Luther Marsh the impact of settlement was more severe, though years of restoration have covered most of the scars. Down to Lake Belwood, the riverscape is still mostly rural.

Fergus and Elora were early mill towns. They have been modernized and old buildings have been repurposed but it is easy to visualize how these towns would have looked 150 years ago. The mills were built to take advantage of the strong—sometimes tumultuous—current of the river in the gorge along this stretch.

After the Elora Gorge, there is another brief dawdle through peaceful countryside until the river enters what is now the urban area of Waterloo, Kitchener, and Cambridge. The two former cities were built somewhat to the west of the river, but Cambridge—an amalgamation of Galt, Preston, and Hespeler—is on both banks, making this the most thoroughly urban part of the Grand.

Below Cambridge the river is tranquil, and there are forested banks and quiet stretches of water. Imagination is needed to reconstruct the industry, mainly mining and logging, that existed here, and the social and commercial activity that that created. We have to picture the steamships and barges passing up and down the river and through the locks and canals, and the towns and mills along them. There would have been wharves and warehouses, and piles of logs waiting to fuel the steamships. There would be towpaths for the horses that pulled the barges. Some remnants of this are visible, but most of them are not eye-catching. Instead we have banks that are farmed or wooded, and some small towns and villages. The river's present-day serenity is modern, post-industrial. Brantford and Paris are the only sizeable urban areas in this stretch; lower down, at Port Maitland, there is some large industry.

And then there is the river's outlet into Lake Erie. As with all river mouths, the interaction with the lake is important in the identity and life of the river here; the voice of the lake is added to the conversation.

The images and text that follow explore and articulate our vision and experience of the river. Each image is like a stone dropped into a pool, generating spreading ripples. The specific leads to the general and back to the specific. Among the planet's rivers, the Grand is both representative and unique.

Though I mention the whole watershed from time to time, we deal only with the main river, and for the most part we stay fairly close to its banks. Yet the rest of the watershed is a ghostly presence because everything connects. In fact, as our project evolved, connectedness became one of its motifs. Present interweaves with past.

By the very nature of his work, Gerard depicts what is visible. I work from what is visible towards what is not—the now-invisible history, the invisible parts of the ecosystem, the resonances, the ripples sent out by each image, from this place and time to elsewhere and elsewhen.

For all this interconnectedness, the spiderweb is an appropriate symbol.

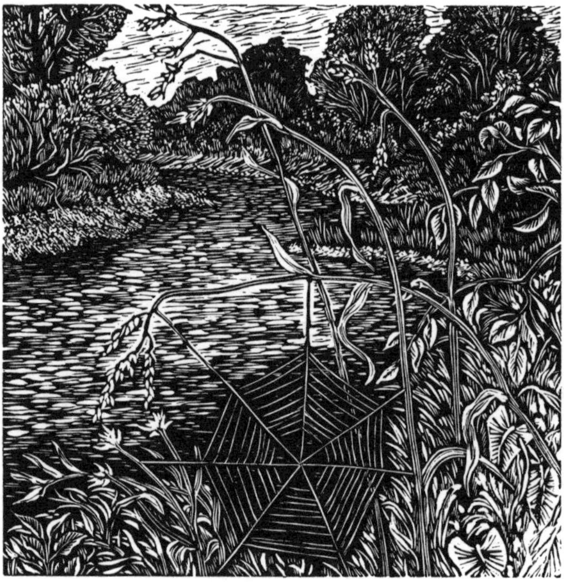

The Essays and The Engravings

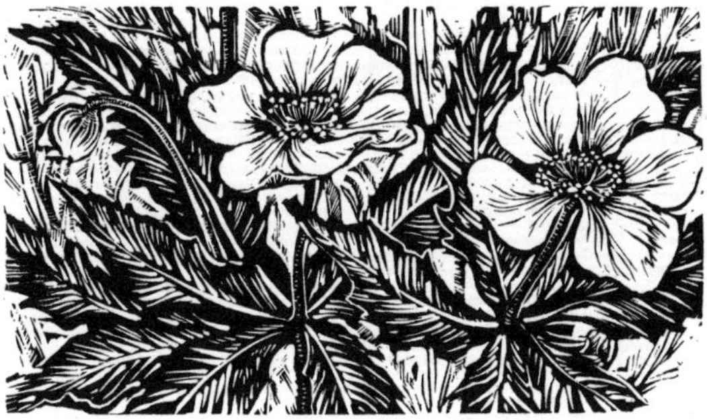

The Grand River starts as a wet spot in a field near Dundalk, Ontario. Then, with the addition of one more drop—rain or dew or melted snow—the water begins to move, trickling downhill.

I find 'watershed' an evocative word, much more so than 'drainage basin', which is the more correct and widely used term. Whichever term is used, what it refers to is an incredibly intricate system of water, soil, and rock (including subterranean levels), of innumerable minute trickles that all find their way downhill. Flowing downhill is what makes water one of the most powerful forces on the planet. It shapes the land—'watershed' means hills and mountains as well as streams—and creates the vegetation and climate that we live within.

Water is intrinsic to weather; most weather involves the presence or absence of water. Water interacts with every element of the vegetation, wildlife, and human lives that it touches. Other than air, nothing is so pervasive in the biosphere, the thin envelope which makes this planet habitable. Our bodies are more than half water: this is where we began.

So this is where the Grand begins. When more drops are added, and other threads of water, it flows a bit faster among the plant stems, visible only to the small creatures that live there. These are the first syllables of its dialogue with the land. Very soon the stream begins to make a riverbed, to acquire banks. It grows into a creek big enough so that at its intersection with a road there is a culvert. Other creeks merge with it: it is now part of a watershed.

Gerard and I were here on the summer solstice. There were swallows, mosquitoes, and deerflies. It was a deeply tranquil scene.

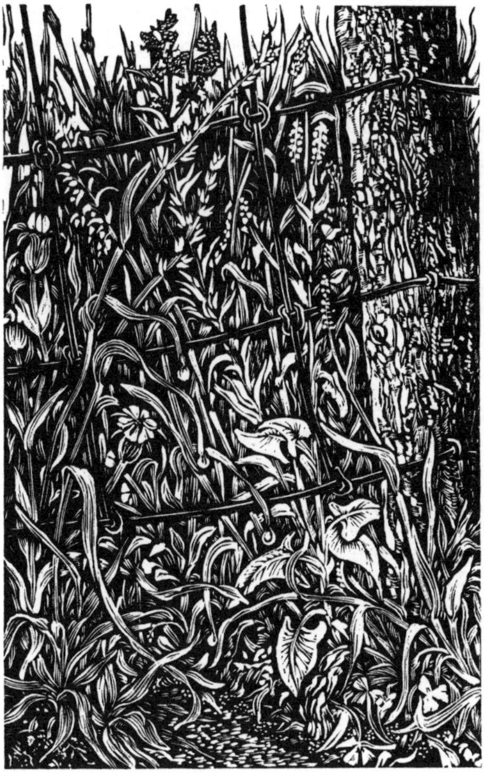

Source of the Grand

By the time it reaches Keldon, the Grand is ten metres wide; the road to this spot is narrow and gravelled, the kind that served farm country for many decades before asphalt became common.

Today the river's water undulates smoothly except where barely emerging stones and a few rushes and yellow pond lilies break the surface into riffles. On the banks grow ferns, horsetails, burrs, and blue irises. There are butterflies and horseflies, and insects invisible to us whose presence is indicated by scooping swallows. The tree trunks in this image are the visible parts of submerged networks of roots that, constantly growing and decaying, are integral to the life of the watershed.

It's an overcast day, the air humid, the bluish-purple clouds suggesting that it might rain. The clouds are airborne water made visible—their flow across the sky is simply another form of river, as is the invisible aquifer. I thought about the hydrological cycle that makes all life possible: evaporation to clouds to rain to river to evaporation. I was part of the cycle, drinking from my water bottle, exhaling moisture that would ultimately condense and drop.

There's a bridge here, an old iron bridge with a wooden deck that rattles under feet and wheels. On it, flattened lumps of horse manure indicate that Mennonites with horse-drawn buggies regularly use it; our lives for a moment intersect with theirs. Gerard and I, having grown up on a farm where a horse pulled the vehicles and farm equipment, remember horse manure well.

Above the cloud cover, two airliners fly over, carrying people whose lives also briefly cross ours.

There is the feel of past habitation, of hard labour, of history, in some posts and bits of wire fencing that no longer keep anything in or out. The silence, barely interrupted by the voice of an invisible bullfrog, is like a taproot into the past. It's an ancient silence, and it suggests great peace and harmony.

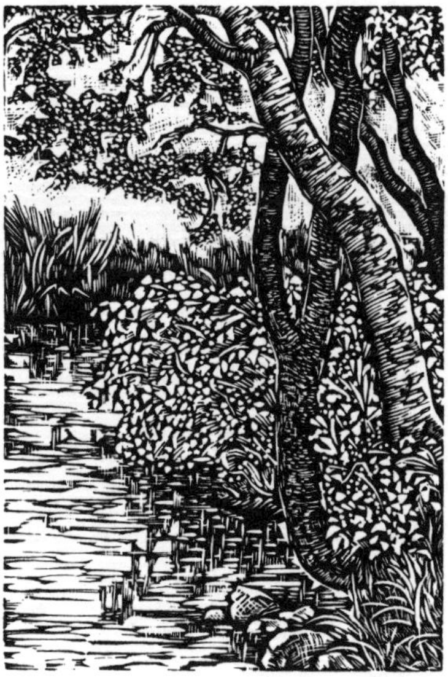

Bankside

This building is another taproot, one that reaches down into the lives of people who came here because, for millennia, the river had been transforming a raw post-glacier landscape into a home. The cabin was built from trees that had been watered by the river, a metamorphosis of water into wood into dwelling that is one of the many ways in which human lives interweave with the rest of the ecosystem. Thinking about the life of the river and the all-pervasive importance of water is one of the routes into a meditation—both practical and spiritual—about ecology and the planet.

This small house also evokes the life of a pioneer family. Although it's a step up from the typical first shanty, it's still very small. The river, just out of sight to the right of the picture, would likely have been the source of water for the household and farm: we can almost see family members walking a well-worn path to fetch water, and the livestock trudging down to drink. Especially for the children, carrying water and firewood was a daily activity, contributing to the family's survival.

Across the road from this little house is a modern farm. Its well is yet another taproot, sunk down to levels where the groundwater and the river's water connect.

Gerard and I were here in March, on the cusp of spring. The snow melting off the south-facing slopes was, invisibly, draining into the river; the steady wind, even though it came from the south, was chilled by the cold soil and the remaining snow. It carried the smell of the cattle in a field across the road, a smell that for ages has meant the production of meat and milk, leather and fertilizer, the stuff of life. The air was soft with the coming of spring.

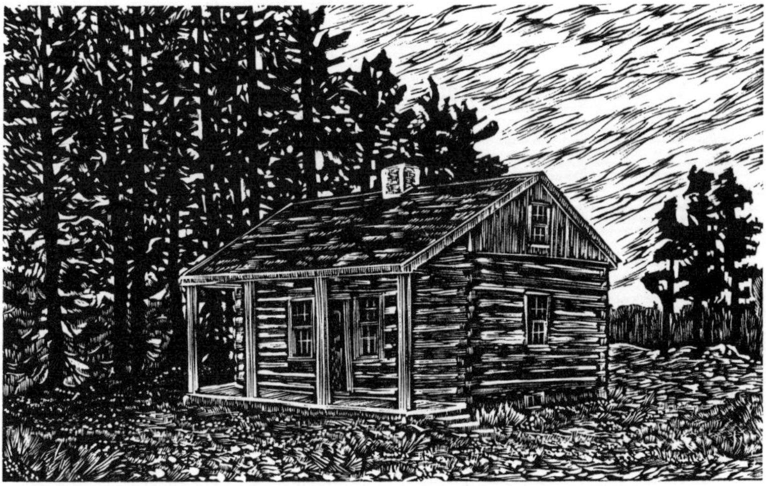

Log House near Monticello

The Grand's upper reaches are mainly farm country; in fact, about eighty percent of the watershed is rural. This engraving reminds us of how most parts of the valley would have looked before the coming of big industries, big highways, subdivisions, and malls.

We tend to construct our image of pioneer life from the buildings and artifacts that the early settlers left behind, but a cleared field is just as much an artifact as a building is, or a quilt, or a wooden rake. For the settler, a cleared field would be a huge achievement, taking years to complete. Imagine his satisfaction when the last stump was gone, when he could finally drive his team and plough back and forth to make neat, straight furrows. His house would be enormously important to him and his family, but the field would have been a much bigger accomplishment.

We view the scene with different eyes. The engraving shows the contrast between the forest that maintained the healthy life of the river valley and the cleared field representing the watershed-wide deforestation that upset the valley's life. The fringe of small trees and grasses along the fence is, however, the kind of buffer that helps to reduce the discharge of agricultural chemicals into the river. Present-day landowners are encouraged to preserve or restore such buffers.

Yet we can understand that the first farmers, who needed to grow food for their families, could not afford to preserve more than just enough trees to supply wood for building and fuel.

We can understand, more than the pioneers did, the watershed's interconnectedness. Both the woods and the field are nourished by the river, and both are essential parts of a watershed that is now home to nearly a million people.

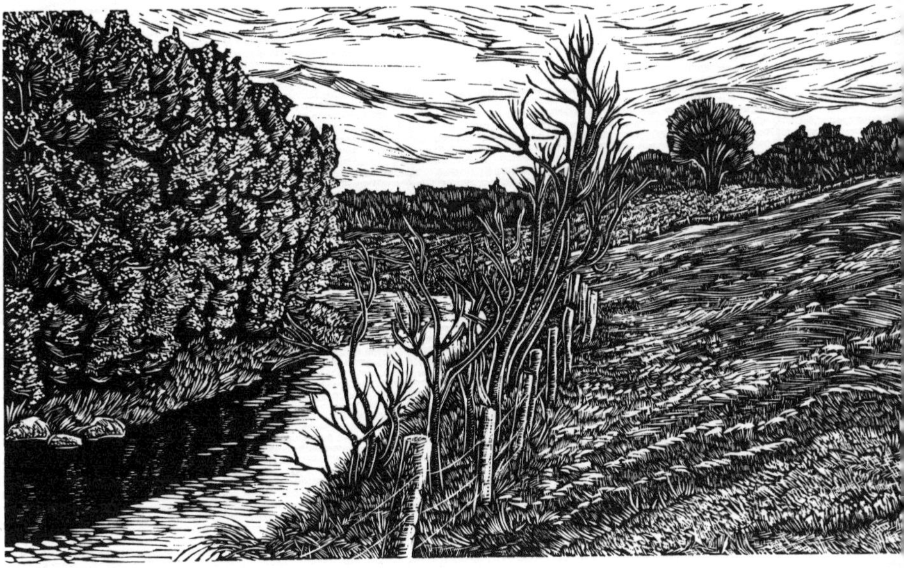

Fields Sloping to the River

This is one of the faces—and phases—of the river: some of its water has become ice. The dialogue of land and water along the banks is, for a season, inaudible.

This is an image that nudges you into thinking about what's invisible. When looking at a frozen river one reflects on the current that continues running under the ice, the animals and plants living there, the continuous slow shifting of stones and sand, the work of river-making that never stops.

Under the snow-cover on the field and in the woods on the horizon, life continues—and also on the farm to which this field belongs. The nineteenth-century farmer would be busy with the winter farm work—hauling logs out of the woodlot, sawing and chopping firewood, tending the livestock, repairing the harness and wooden implements, going to market with produce like apples, cabbages, root vegetables, and dairy products. The woman and the children would be spinning and knitting and mending, keeping the fires burning and the family fed.

And, in earlier days, they would all be dealing with the stresses of living through a long winter in a small cabin. In summer they would be outdoors most of the day, but in winter they'd be inside. The cabin would be crowded. A bad storm keeping everyone indoors, a crying baby, a sick family member, insufficient food, the impossibility of washing and drying clothes and linen properly—those conditions were major trials for the early settlers.

That made it all the more fortunate that, surprisingly, winter was a good time for travelling. Snow made a much better road surface than did the mud and dust and ruts and washboard of the other seasons. It would have been liberating to travel in a sleigh, with comparative ease and speed, and to be away, even for an afternoon or evening, from the constant work and the confined living space.

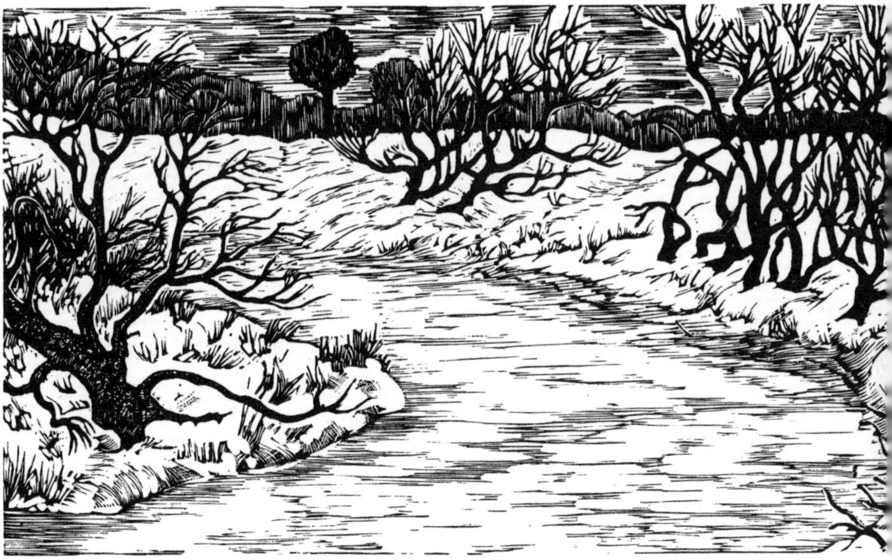

The River Silenced by Winter

The breaking up of the ice in spring is one of the fastest and most dramatic metamorphoses in the life of a river. The stream in spate—snow and ice transformed back into tumultuous water—sometimes causes damage, but it is only humans who call it damage when their works are destroyed. In the life of the river, it's part of the natural cycle.

All the same, the engraving depicts what, in the late nineteenth and early twentieth centuries, would be the beginning of downstream flooding. It's the spring runoff from a cleared field like this that, during bad floods, ended up in the streets and basements of Bridgeport and Galt and Brantford. Now such flooding is much reduced: the surplus water is held in reservoirs and then released in the summer when it's needed.

The farm depicted is well past the pioneering phase though this is still family farming, not yet agribusiness. Allowing for regional differences in the look of the land and the design of the buildings, this image could represent thousands of Canadian farms, deeply rooted in the landscape and the human and natural ecosystem of the area.

This peaceful scene evokes thoughts of very early spring, a season when the weather and the appearance of the landscape change day by day. The nineteenth-century farmer, going to the kitchen for his midday dinner, might remark to his wife, 'River's high, ice going out fast.' And he might add, 'Quite a bit of warmth in the sun today. Saw the first snowdrop.' It's a season marked by firsts: the first pussy willows, the first robin. Warm climates don't know this season.

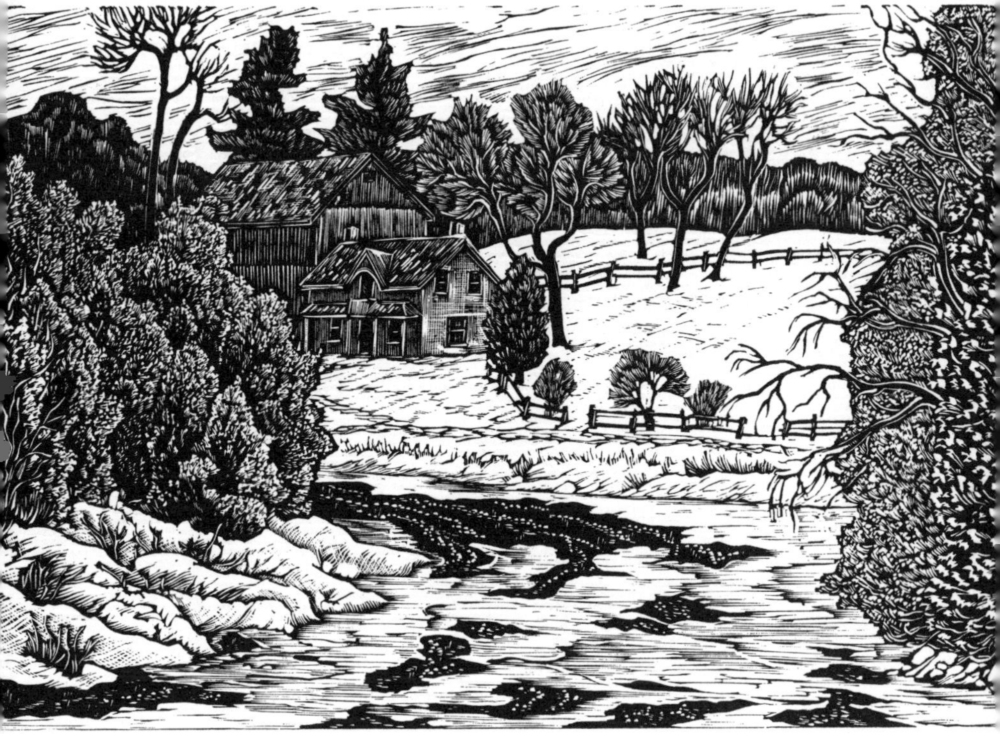

End of Winter on the Upper Grand River

The early-April day when Gerard made the sketch for this engraving was cold and misty but the air was soft. Above the cloud cover geese flew north, honking. We were parked on a gravel road near some fragments of fence—decaying wooden posts, sagging and intermittent wire mesh. The land felt ancient and glacier-worn, and the gaunt trees enhanced that mood. The scene evoked northern Canada, which is not surprising because parts of the Luther Marsh support vegetation typical of boreal forest, and the whole area has a climate similar to that of Algonquin Park.

Luther Marsh is one of the most important headwaters of the Grand River, and is a wetland of major significance. To pioneers, however, it was an obstacle; it was not until 1853 that the first serious settlement took place here. The land, having poor natural drainage, was not good for farming. So the settlers turned to logging, assisted by hundreds of experienced lumbermen brought in by the government. The logs were floated downstream—very Canadian.

The clearing of the forest, however, contributed to severe flooding lower down the valley.

After a bad forest fire in the early 1870s, renewed efforts were made to farm the land. Drainage ditches were dug and the area became known for hay production and horse breeding. But the ditches poured more water into the river, aggravating the disastrous fluctuations of water levels, and in 1952 a dam was constructed across Black Creek, at the mouth of the marsh, to regulate the water flow.

The whole marsh—its ecological importance now very well appreciated, and likely to be of increasing value in an era of climate change—is currently managed through the co-operation of the Grand River Conservation Authority, the Ontario Ministry of Natural Resources, Ducks Unlimited, and other concerned organizations.

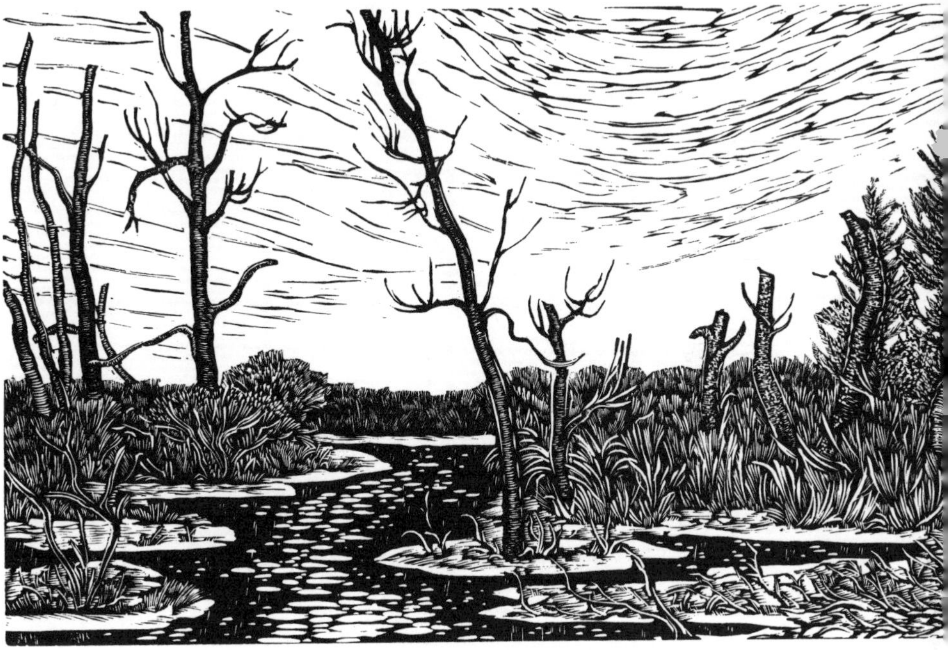

Spring Thaw, Luther Marsh

The Luther Marsh Wildlife Management Area, which was created by the Black Creek dam, encompasses some 5,600 hectares comprising the Luther Lake reservoir surrounded by swamps, bogs, meadows, plantations, natural forests, fields, and croplands. The area is a raised plateau; because of its high elevation in the Dundalk Uplands, it is the source of a number of creeks that flow into the Grand and its tributaries. The climate is cool and in a few hollows there is wetland vegetation resembling that of the muskeg of the boreal forest.

These features provide habitat for a great variety of wildlife. The area attracts enormous numbers of migratory and nesting birds; 246 species have been recorded, and 132 of those are breeding. Because of the habitat's features, a number of western Canadian species have moved into Ontario and spread from the Luther Marsh to other locations in the province. There are also such mammals, amphibians, reptiles, and fish as are comfortable in the region's diverse habitats and range of native and exotic vegetation.

The marsh—besides functioning as a reservoir—is used for wildlife viewing, canoeing, biking, hunting, fishing, and walking, as well as for educational purposes. These uses overlie its earlier life and character. Still clearly visible are the municipal drains created in the nineteenth century in an attempt to make the land amenable to farming; they are now regarded as one of the several different kinds of water bodies in the area.

The egret in the image represents all this richness and ecological significance. Gerard—frequently frustrated by the fact that wildlife won't sit still to be sketched—was amazed at how long the bird stayed where it was, perfectly posed to have its portrait taken.

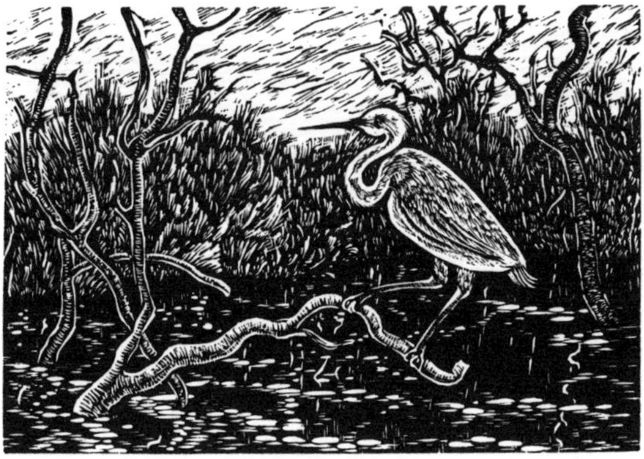

Egret at Luther Marsh

Lake Belwood is an artificial lake, a reservoir behind the Shand Dam, which was built in 1939–42 to control flooding in the spring and augment downstream flow in the dry summer months. The dam now also generates hydroelectricity.

The dam was funded by the federal and provincial governments to put Depression-era unemployed men back to work; when the Second World War began, the project was considered sufficiently important so that work on it was continued and completed. During Hurricane Hazel in 1954 it proved its worth; the cities downstream from it were protected from the kind of damage that Toronto suffered.

While the flood-control function of a dam is of crucial importance, many dams have bad side effects, hampering the movement of fish and impairing water quality. Furthermore, it's now known that a river system benefits from occasional flooding because high water flushes stagnant areas. Many species of aquatic life require an alternation between low and high flows for their life cycle.

Aside from all these important matters of 'plumbing', Belwood is a beautiful lake, twelve kilometres long. Here, on this day, the Grand River's voice is temporarily silent, its current invisible. Also invisible is the wind, though its footprints can be seen in the rippling water and the cloud shadows moving across land and lake. The lake is ringed with cottages and—as shown by the boat in the engraving—is much used for recreation. There is also a conservation area at its southern end.

It was here that Gerard sketched the sandpiper (see p. 3), one small bird wading and dipping in this shallow little bay.

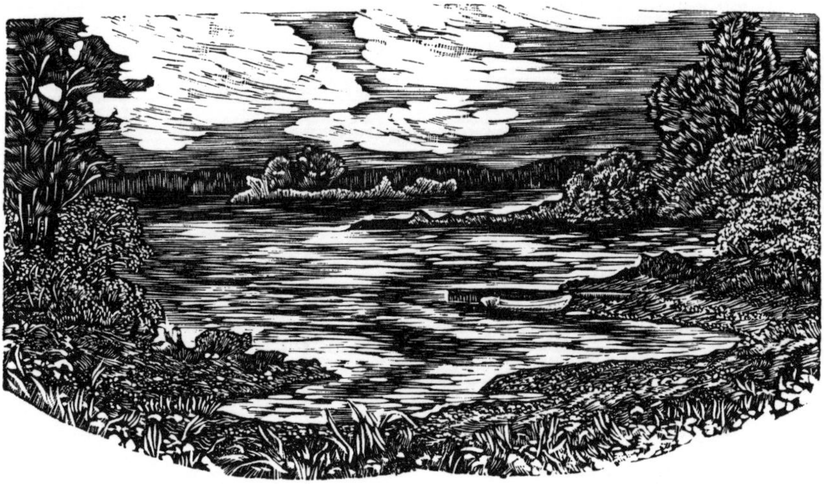

Lake Belwood

The first settlers in what is now the Fergus area were freed Black slaves from the U.S., led by Richard Pierpoint, who arrived as early as 1821. Pierpoint's land was on both sides of the river, just upstream from what became the centre of Fergus. The Black settlement seems to have existed until the late 1840s, by which time speculators and European pioneers had moved in; Pierpoint had left by then, and had died in 1837 or 1838.

In 1833 the Scots came, led by Adam Fergusson and James Webster. Fergus grew into a busy town, its mills using the current of the river, which here flows through a significant gorge. After the railway reached the town in 1870 a variety of industries developed, including a sewing-machine factory, a tannery, a foundry, a brewery, and a planing mill. Because of the presence of both an abundant supply of limestone and a number of skilled masons, many of its residential and commercial buildings were constructed from local stone. Fergus is still a notable 'stone town'.

The post office, however, was faced not with local limestone but with sandstone from a quarry near Caledon in the valley of the Credit River, transported to Fergus by rail. It was constructed in 1911–12, and its impressive appearance reminds us of the central importance of postal services in early communities. Invisible behind the imposing building are decades of a more haphazard mail service—letters and packages carried by a lone horseman or a carrier's cart or a stagecoach. In the early days, everyone living in the area came from somewhere else. Both the settlers and those they had left behind in other towns and countries were eager, even anxious, for news. There was also business mail, and there were newspapers, magazines, and parcels. The postal service maintained a tenuous but invaluable connection with home.

The building, enlarged in the 1950s, still serves as a post office.

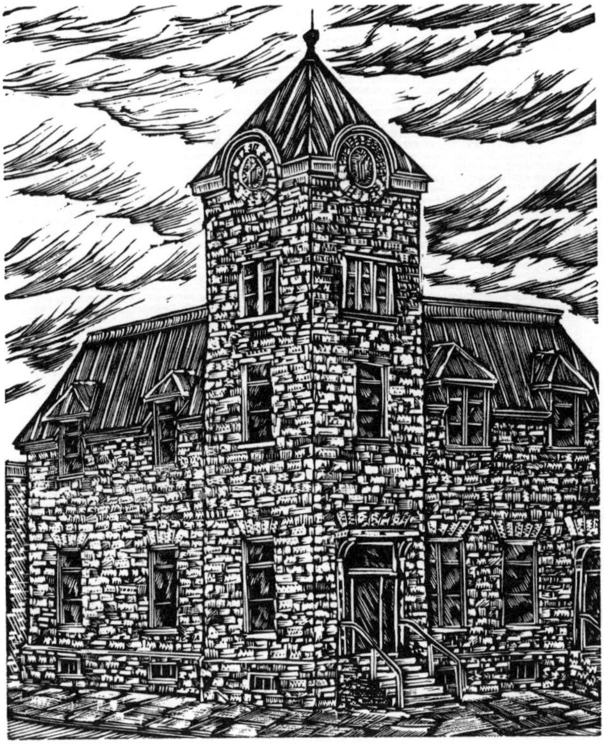

Post Office in Fergus

It was between 1920 and 1934 that John C. Templin, publisher of the *Fergus News-Record*, created a garden on the bank of the Grand River behind the newspaper office on St. Andrew Street. Both he and his wife loved gardens and gardening: out of such modest soil comes this remarkable piece of riverscape. To do the stonework, Templin hired local craftsmen, principally Roger Bricker, a Scottish master mason who had a long history of building with limestone in Fergus.

Templin saw this project as a way of providing employment for his fellow townspeople during the Depression, but he must also have been inspired by the beauty of the gorge. The walls here are not quite as high as those at Elora but they are equally impressive, and when you stand close to the river at this point and, in your mind's eye, review the appearance of the town it's easy to see how the buildings grow out of the stone that underlies the whole landscape and was exposed when the river carved this gorge. Like the gorge, the buildings are geological time made visible.

Originally the gardens were much larger and more elaborate than they are now, and a full-time gardener was employed. There were iron gates on St. Andrew Street and a good-sized garden, made up of lawn, flower borders, shrubs, and a lily pond with a fountain. On the lower level, which is all that survives today, there was a second pond and also birdhouses and a birdbath, benches, a table, and an apple tree. And then there are the steps going down to the water, a wonderfully dramatic way of getting in touch with the Grand River.

The whole stone garden is a blending of the natural and the human-made, a garden fused with and rooted in the river.

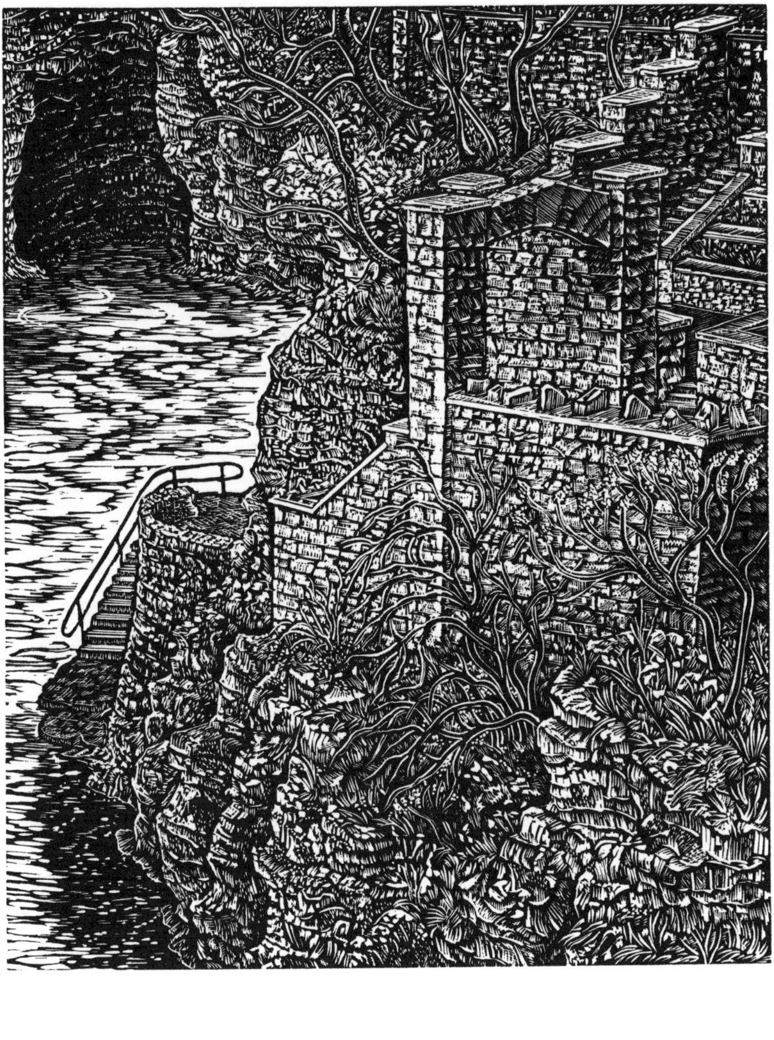

Templin Gardens, Fergus

This image—the scene is just downstream from Fergus—shows the river in spate; in this spot, and on this day, the dialogue of land and water is a vigorous argument. The banks speak of millennia of being gnawed and gouged and sand-blasted by the water: rocks are the river's vocal cords.

The water's action smoothes the rock but also undermines the banks, causing rockfalls, which leave behind rough shapes and surfaces. It is from banks like this that stones and boulders fall into the stream—the boulders that are visible when the water is relatively low and are so characteristic of the river's bed. Some stay in place for decades, perhaps centuries, changing shape as the water works on them. Frost opens fissures, fragments break off.

In turn, the boulders direct the flow of the water, forming pools and rapids, creating environments for water creatures and plants. There they lie until a major flood shifts them. So there is constant change in the riverbed: sand particles in perpetual movement, driven along the bottom or suspended in the water; larger pebbles and stones and boulders shifting whenever the current is strong enough. This is the life of the river, and it can be a turbulent one. In our imagination we can for a moment be the fish that lives in this environment.

And we can be one of the cedar trees that have chosen to grow on this spot—to our eyes an unpromising and even perilous location. Their presence gives us insight into the river's relationship to the vegetation on its banks: each challenges the other in a state of what can be either balance or struggle but is always part of the dialogue.

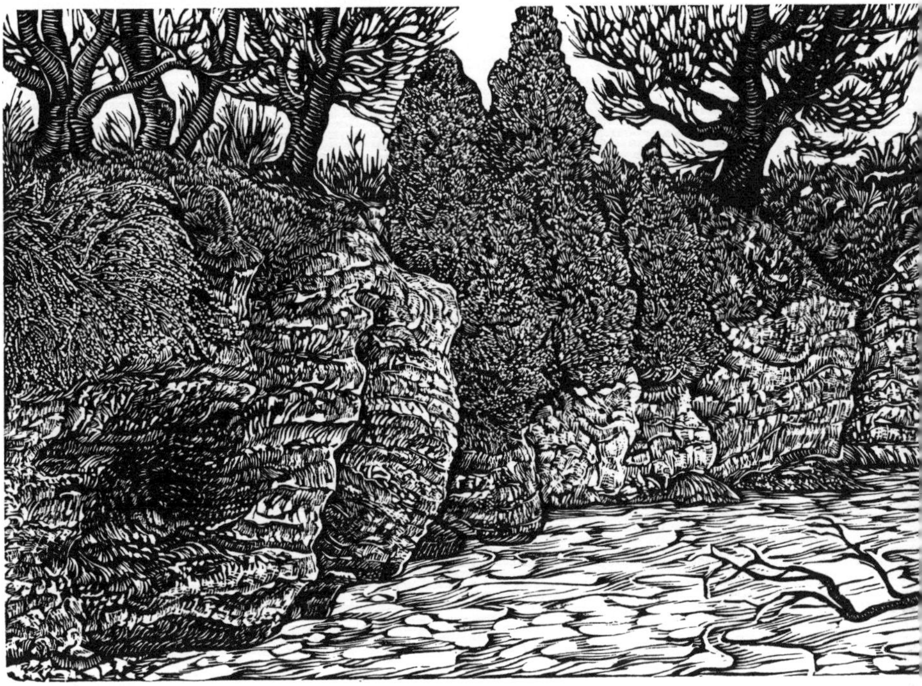

Eroded Rocks near Fergus

In Elora, the river is a pervasive presence, sometimes rushing and sometimes almost idling through its gorge. The area was sacred to First Peoples, and the Neutral nation, after their defeat by the Iroquois in 1651, took refuge in caves in the gorge's cliffs.

The power of the river's current attracted Roswell Matthews who, starting in 1817, tried to build a mill to harness that power, but it defeated his attempts by destroying his dam every spring until he gave up. The settlement was actually founded in 1832 by Captain William Gilkison, a cousin of John Galt, and it became a centre for the surrounding countryside.

The first successful mill on this site was a flour mill that was built in 1850 but burned in 1859. It was immediately rebuilt, using stone from the gorge, and therefore the building has its roots deep in the geology of the area, just as the water power that drove the mill machinery links it inextricably with the life of the Grand. That building is one of the focal points of the village. Until 1972 it was a fully functioning water mill, one of the largest on the river. After that it became a notable inn and restaurant. At that time the penstock—the pipe delivering water to power the mill—still conveyed water from the pond above the mill to a small hydroelectric plant at its base.

The gorge, together with the many historic buildings, make Elora popular with visitors.

Because the village is a place of cliffs, it's interesting to see that when settlers began building they created another kind of cliff, as depicted in the engraving—habitations producing a visual effect similar to the one created by the towering and overhanging stone walls of the gorge.

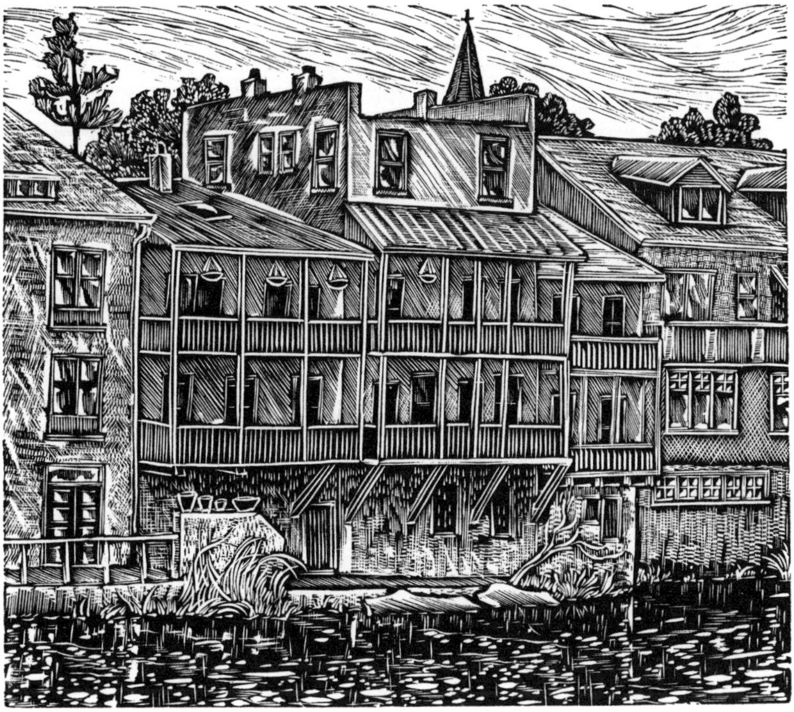

Grand River at Elora

One reason for the designation of the Grand as a Heritage River is the Elora Gorge. Between high walls the river thunders over cataracts and eats away at the banks, or meanders quietly in level stretches. In flood, it can fill its bed between the cliffs, though at low water there are shoals and exposed, much-eroded rocks.

The bedrock through which the gorge is carved was formed about 410 million years ago and consists largely of fossils laid down on the floor of an ancient sea. The strata are almost horizontal and clearly visible; they contribute to both the geological importance and the visual appeal of the gorge. The cliffs, which are about thirty metres high, are remarkable for the overhangs caused by the erosion of the somewhat softer stone underneath.

The creation of the gorge is to a considerable extent the result of big events such as rockfalls and floods. But the much less dramatic work of gorge-making is a continuous process of erosion, including the gentle but implacable digging of the vegetation's roots. The cedars and other trees clinging to the very edge contribute to this process and, though high on top of the cliffs, are part of the life of the river.

As in many parts of the watershed, early settlers cut down practically all of the forest; here, they left only the narrowest fringe of trees along the rim of the gorge. Much of what we see now is the result of replanting; the area is greener now than it was then.

Gerard and I, on the day when this sketch was made, were in the Elora Gorge Conservation Area. Gerard was facing Lover's Leap, the outlook point at the junction of the Grand River and Irvine Creek. While he was sketching, some gulls flew along the gorge below us, startlingly white against the darker shades of rock and water. To see flying birds from above is always a remarkable experience.

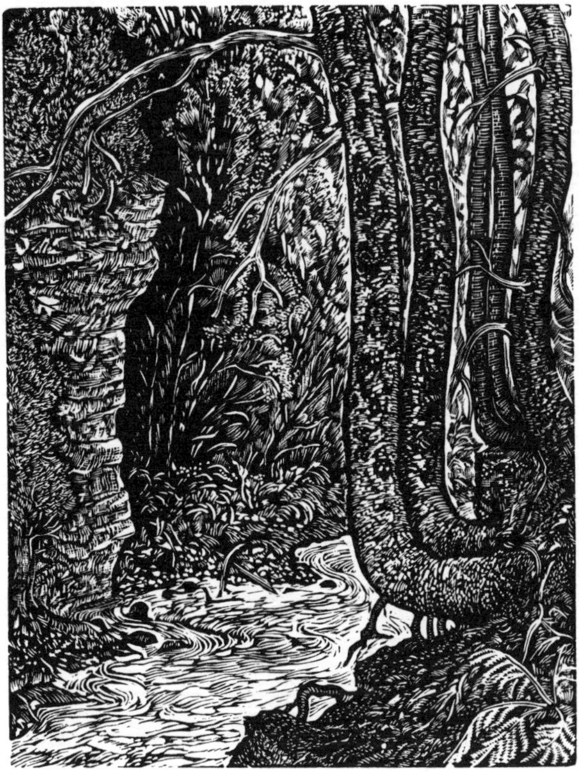

Elora Gorge

At water level, in the Elora Gorge, the river has a very different feel than it does when viewed from above. The cliffs are high and in many places overhanging, but the depth of the gorge is not as insistently present to the senses: rather one focuses on the river and its bed, on the banks and boulders where water and rock meet. The human visitor sees the place from the river's point of view: for it, the upper levels of the cliffs are no longer relevant, except when there are rockfalls. Thousands of years have passed since it worked on them, and it is now busy with other tasks of river-making.

The river is used for many recreational purposes, such as walking, fishing, camping, and whitewater rafting. It is along these rock faces that David Boyle, mentioned in the introduction, acquired his practical education in geology, and since then the area has been extensively studied by scientists. Even the non-specialist can see that the rock walls are geology laid open to view, legible to those able to read the language.

The path by which we descended to the river here is now in the Elora Conservation Area but was formerly part of a farm. It was the only place in the gorge where cattle could go to the river to drink. To make my cautious way down to the river and back up again, I had to negotiate steep slopes of hard-packed earth interrupted by small outcrops of stone like sporadic—but not nearly frequent enough—footholds. It was almost impossible to imagine cattle with their ponderous gait and swaying udders doing it, but apparently they did. This is yet another way in which the river was interconnected with the animal and human life on its banks.

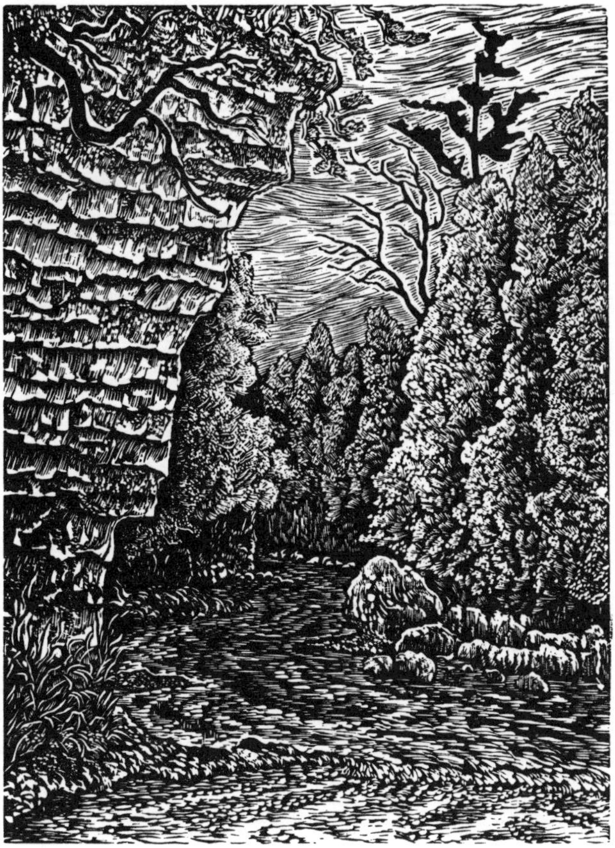

Rock Face in the Elora Gorge

This stretch—just below the gorge—is a tranquil place where, on this summer day, the river flows gently between wooded banks. It's a good spot for getting close to the river itself, with almost no distractions from the works of man except the small road and an elderly bridge. You can sit here for quite a while without seeing another soul or hearing anything except the water's murmur and the call of a bird. This is the essence of peaceful riverness, a place for meditation and healing and for artistic creation. Watching the flowing water can mesmerize you into serenity.

There's a small island in the river here, one of the intermittent islands that exist when the water is low and are submerged at other times. It supports vegetation, perhaps not in spite of its periodic submersion but because of it. That island is a miniature ecological niche in the whole complex life of the river where these particular plants are at home.

When Gerard was close to the water doing the drawing for this image, he noticed that there were many small fish in the shallows. He called me over, and together we squatted on the bank like a couple of little kids, observing the beautiful fish darting across the gravel of the riverbed.

Over our heads was a bridge, which, I learned later in the course of my research, has a bit of a history. There has been a bridge here since 1845. The present one—Chamber's Bridge—is a Camelback Pratt Through Truss bridge. Because there is a superfluous pier that is not needed to support the present structure, it's possible that the superstructure was brought to this location from elsewhere in 1946. Besides carrying local traffic, it also provides a river crossing for the Grand Valley Trail.

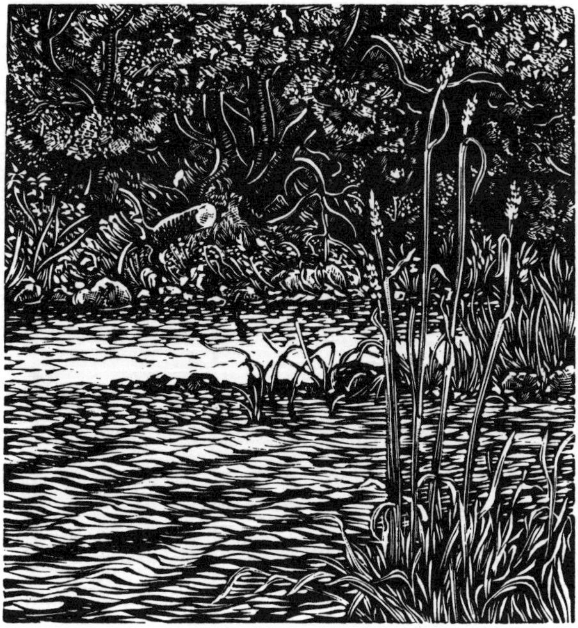

Near Inverhaugh

Bridges are places where road and river intersect and where the banks are linked. Accustomed as we are to having bridges almost wherever we need them, we rarely reflect on what a drastic barrier a bridge-less and unfordable stretch of river could be to pioneers, not only in the initial journey to their farm-to-be but in daily life, separating them from mills and stores and churches; the fact that settlements so often arose near bridges indicates their importance.

This covered bridge at West Montrose, built in 1881 and now the last old one remaining in Ontario, speaks of the pioneer farms and communities that it joined: 'between' is a word of connection as well as of separation.

The bridge is sixty-two metres long. The roof and walls protect the bridge's structure and have contributed to its long life; it is carefully maintained for its heritage value and attracts visitors from all over the world.

A few years ago an application was made to Woolwich Township to open a gravel quarry at a site within two hundred metres of the bridge. The townspeople's opposition and other factors led to the cancellation of the project.

Along with this successful campaign has come the designation of the area as a Cultural Heritage Landscape. Many attributes combine to make it qualify. While the bridge is central, the description given in the designation also includes buildings, cemeteries, the village layout, and farms (building clusters and fields), all of which are visible records of the lives of the Scottish and Mennonite settlers. The area is also, and specifically, designated for views of the valley and bridge, and for the lifeways of the Old Order Mennonite culture.

In formulating the concept of a Cultural Heritage Landscape, UNESCO recognized the importance of entire complexes of natural and human-made significance and beauty. West Montrose's whole heritage is worth protecting for its economic, environmental, and social benefits.

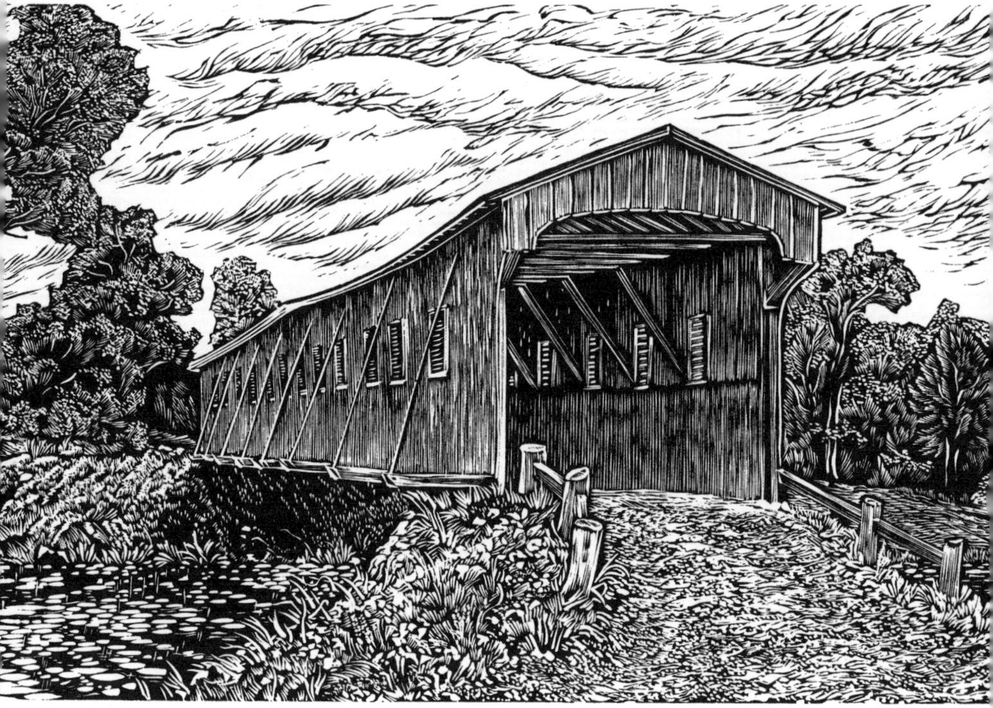

Covered Bridge

Winterbourne is one of those villages that show vestiges of their earlier selves. A busy road partly spoils the historic feel, but when Gerard and I set out on foot we found whiffs of the past. The land, the buildings, and the layout of the village remember the past—as does the river with its timeless presence.

On the north edge of Winterbourne, Cox's Creek enters the Grand, and just north of that there was once a Black settlement named Colbornesburg. Freed slaves, persecuted in Ohio, petitioned the Executive Council of Upper Canada for land. They were denied twice, but then Lieutenant Governor Sir John Colborne encouraged them to come. Paola Brown led the group to the Winterbourne area in about 1829. By 1832 they had a church and schoolhouse. Thirty-four Blacks are known to have settled there, but by 1837 most had moved away.

The man who gave his name to the creek was Michael Cox, a blacksmith who set up shop about 1840. The founding of this second village is, however, attributed to William Lanphier; Winterbourne was the name of his family home in Scotland. On the creek, Lanphier built a dam and a sawmill and gristmill. The village soon had a general store and a carriage factory, a school, and two churches, Presbyterian and Methodist. It was rooted in the riverscape at the mouth of the creek.

The blacksmith shop depicted in the engraving was almost certainly not Cox's, but it is an interesting structure with its round-arched entrance, varied windows, and handsome masonry work.

Blacksmiths, besides shoeing horses, made and repaired tools, household objects, wheel-rims, nails and hinges, hammers and axes, the metal parts of wagons and carriages and harness, and innumerable other metal objects. The railway, when it came, brought this merchandise from urban factories, and local manufacture ended, but a building like this reminds us of the craftsmen and the community they served.

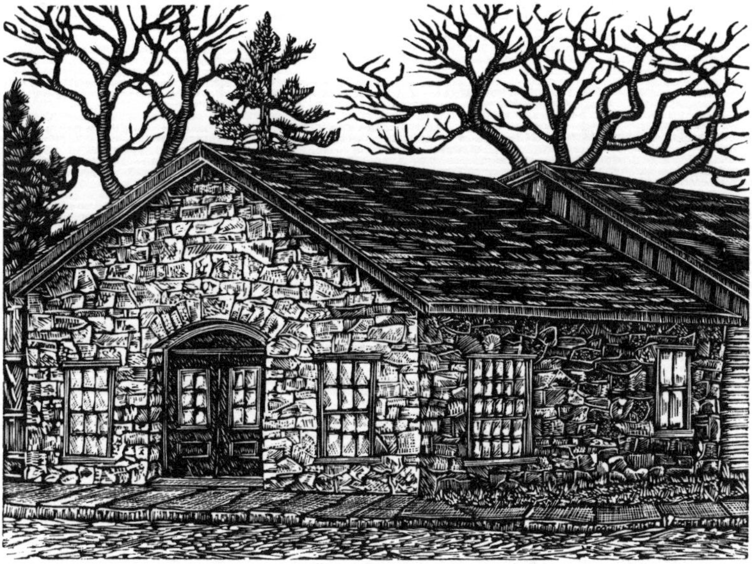

Blacksmith Shop, Winterbourne

The Conestoga wagon is the emblem of the migration of Mennonites and others (such as Germans) who came from Pennsylvania. Vehicles like this had long been used to carry freight along the eastern seaboard of the United States. The wagon's floor curved upward at the ends to keep the contents from shifting, and cracks in the body were sealed with tar so that the wagon could be used as a boat when there were rivers to cross. An average-sized Conestoga wagon could carry up to 5,500 kilograms of cargo and was pulled by as many as eight horses or a dozen oxen.

The Mennonites differed from most other migrants who came to Upper Canada in that they were not refugees in the same sense as the United Empire Loyalists were. They chose to emigrate because they were looking for more land and more freedom, and they brought goods, livestock, and sometimes financial assets as well as invaluable farming skills and experience. The wagon and team indicate that at least some of them were people of substance. The engraving shows examples of the equipment they would have brought, including a washtub, a stove and a cooking pot, a saw and a hammer, pails and boxes and barrels. A grease pail hangs from the underside of the wagon.

It was a difficult trip. In the early years of the nineteenth century, when the first Mennonites came, roads were virtually nonexistent. The Allegheny Mountains, the Niagara River, and the Beverley Swamp (near what is now Hamilton, Ontario) were huge obstacles. The journey from Pennsylvania could take as long as seven weeks and sometimes involved dismantling the wagons and carrying the parts and the contents past or across an obstacle.

The Mennonites often travelled in groups, which provided help on the journey and created an instant community when they arrived. Most of them settled in the Waterloo area, where they are still a visible and respected presence.

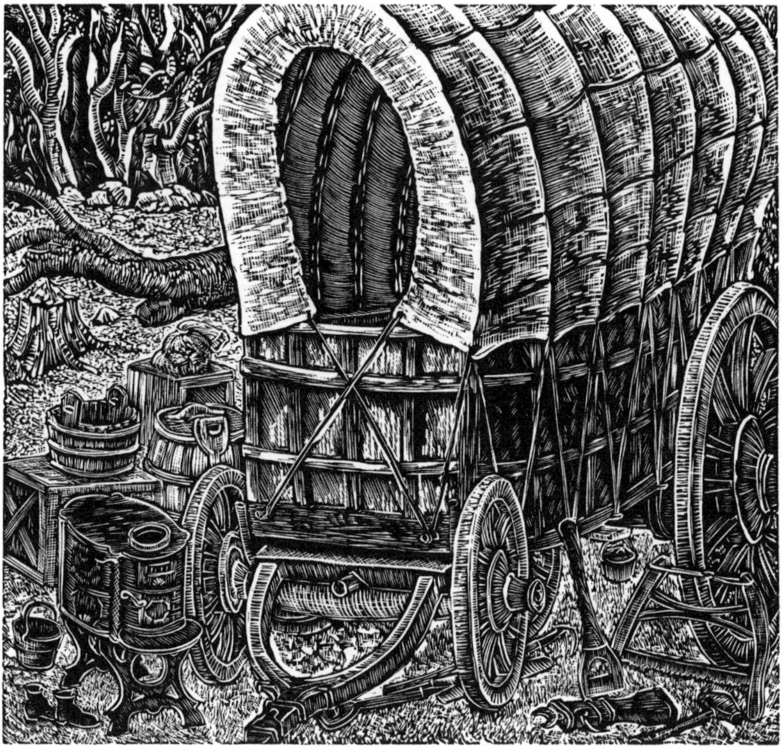

Unloading the Conestoga Wagon

The agriculture that was and is so important along the river is represented by the tools in this engraving: a rake, a scythe with cradle attached (to catch the hay or grain as it fell), and a hay fork. Being grain-related implements, they are linked in function to the bakehouse against which they are displayed. Except for the scythe blade, everything is of wood. Wooden tools could be—and no doubt often were—made at home, along with other wooden objects such as household utensils, furniture, and toys. Lathe-turned objects were probably made by craftsmen, but very simple lathes could be made at home. Creating these objects would be easy for someone with the many skills needed to operate a pioneer farm.

When we picture the settler making these implements, perhaps working by the fireplace on a winter day, we realize that likely it would be he himself and his family who would use them.

Supplementing the settlers' own skills was the work of local craftsmen such as blacksmiths. The tools helped—as much as the river itself did—to create the landscape of the valley. Axes and saws and agricultural implements were essential to the work of clearing land, constructing buildings, and growing food and livestock feed.

The tools are different nowadays but the farming continues. The Grand River watershed contains much fine farmland, producing large amounts of food. But there are uncertainties in the future. Climate change, through its effects on weather, soil, and water, will have a serious impact on agriculture; as I mentioned in the introduction, one of the watchwords in the management of the watershed's resources is resilience, which will make it more possible for nature and humans to adapt to changes.

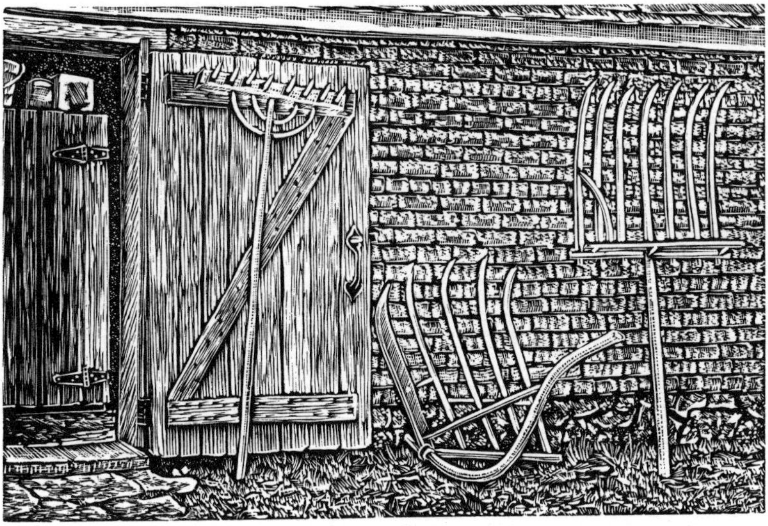

Harvest Tools at a Farm Bakehouse

This small kitchen dresser is at the Joseph Schneider Haus in Kitchener, Ontario. Gerard uses it as the setting for an array of household utensils. On the top shelf are an earthenware pitcher and fruit jar, a tin funnel and tinderbox, and a fruit-picking basket. The middle shelf holds a wooden butter paddle and a pot scraper. Below that: an earthenware jug, a wooden piggin (used for ladling, scooping, etc.), a pestle of turned wood, and a spoon, knife, and fork. Against the side hangs a tin dipper for taking water from a pail. These objects would be made by local craftspeople: the tin objects by a tinsmith, the piggin by a cooper, and the smaller wooden objects by almost anyone.

The earthenware may be the work of William Eby, owner of a pottery that operated from 1856 to 1900 near Conestogo, close to the Grand. Eby produced everyday utensils—crocks, pitchers, jugs, pie plates, flower pots, chamber pots, spittoons—but also whimsical objects like tiny crocks three inches high, small vases and pitchers, and miniature jugs to serve as watch-chain ornaments. He was a Mennonite and, like other Mennonite craftsmen, did not sign his work. It was shards found during a 1967 excavation of the site by the Royal Ontario Museum that enabled existing pots to be identified as his.

The shapes of Eby's pots are standard but the glazes are individual. His only resources for glazes were iron and copper, and the lead linings from tea boxes. The modern Ontario potter Helen Brink writes: 'What is most remarkable is the living quality of almost every glaze he used. They and the clay are so well married that each enhances the other, rather than the glaze acting as a cover to hide the clay.... The glaze is relatively thin, crazing finely when the major flux was lead and softly matt [*sic*] when an iron slip was used.'

The clay came from nearby St. Clement's: the pots are rooted in the valley's soil.

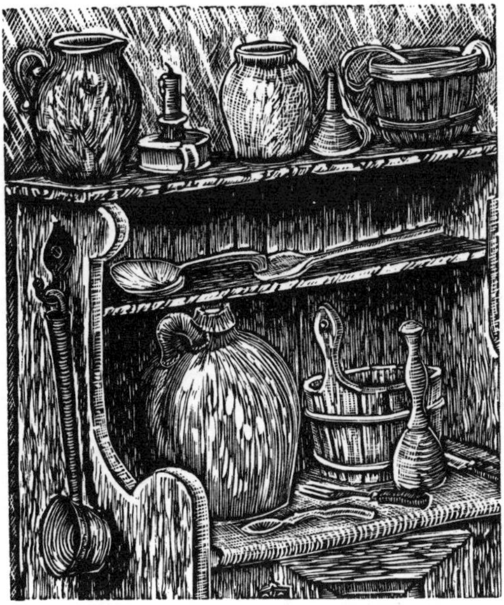

Pioneer Kitchen Dresser

Here the Grand River is joined by the Conestogo; the actual junction is out of sight, just beyond the road that runs on the far side of the house. The hilly terrain depicted in the image reminds us that watersheds are about land as well as water.

The first occupants of this land were Captain Thomas Smith and his wife, who came from Vermont. They built a two-storey, seven-room log house and were well-known for their hospitality. It's believed that the first European child born in Woolwich Township was their daughter Priscilla in 1808.

After the Smiths moved away, the property was bought by Conrad Stroh in 1854. The family first lived in the log house, which was not demolished until 1911–12, but in 1859 Conrad built the brick one shown in the engraving. Though the Strohs came from Germany, the square windows under the roof show Mennonite influence.

About 1870 the eighty-one-hectare farm was divided between two of Conrad's sons, George and Jacob. George's youngest son was Walter, and the house is at present owned and occupied by Louise Stroh, widow of Walter's son, the late Reverend Donald Stroh.

Don was born in the village of Conestogo, a mile west of here, in a house in which his and Louise's daughter now lives. As a boy he constantly visited the house in the engraving, then occupied by his two uncles and an aunt. The uncles and Don's father farmed the land, but one uncle was also the township clerk and the other owned the grocery store, as well as operating a small printing press on which he did printing jobs for the town.

In Don's scrapbook about the locality, I discovered a note in Don's handwriting saying that William Lyon Mackenzie King, growing up in Kitchener (see p. 82), frequently came to this spot to fish.

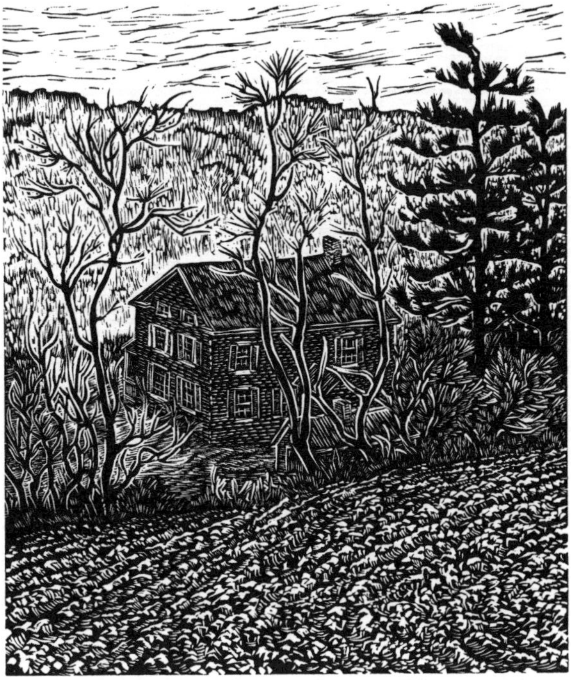

Overlooking the Grand River Valley

Just downstream from Bridgeport are the remains of two bridge piers, a tall one that is unmistakably a pier and, near it, what looks like a pile of rocks but, as the alignment and an aerial view make clear, is another pier, more severely damaged by ice floes, floods, and all the other buffetings of more than a century of the river's life. They were the beginnings of a bridge that was never completed.

Following the development of hydroelectric power from Niagara Falls, there was a surge of interest in electrically powered railways, both urban and interurban, and several came into existence along the Grand River. Sir Adam Beck was one of the principal promoters. The project most affecting the Berlin (Kitchener) area was the Peoples Railway, a network that, according to ambitious plans, would have been anchored by Stratford and Woodstock in the west and would have spread as far east as Guelph. Organization and fundraising started in 1908, and then construction work was begun, mostly west of Berlin. The route was surveyed, embankments were made, and bridges were built over small creeks and gullies. Piers were erected in the Grand River just downstream from Bridgeport. The ones depicted in the engraving are easily visible, and there are also several to the east, on what is now dry land; in the river's earlier, flood-prone years, they would have supported a longer bridge striding across land that was frequently flooded.

Initial financing was provided by the Bugg brothers of Stratford, but eventually their funds ran out and no rail was ever laid.

Most historical remains are of structures that were completed and had a reasonable life span. But historical narrative also includes projects and endeavours that did not, like the Peoples Railway.

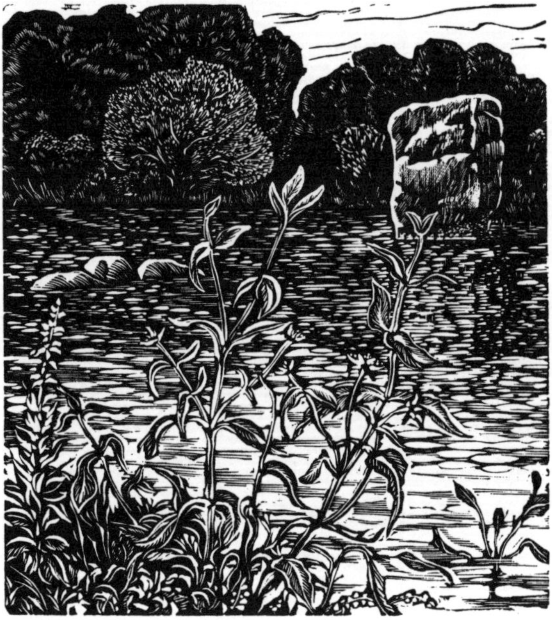

Remnants of a Bridge

The core of what is now the city of Waterloo was built on the farm of Abraham Erb, who arrived in the area from Pennsylvania in 1806. In 1808 he built a sawmill on a tributary of the Grand that ran through his property, and in 1816 he added a gristmill. The village that grew up was, in 1816, named Waterloo. Erb did more than establish mills: in a time when there were no hotels, he provided accommodation in the basement of his gristmill for the farmers who brought their grain for grinding, and he also trained and employed a considerable number of Pennsylvania immigrants.

The settlement's first schoolhouse—depicted in this engraving—was built in 1820 on his farm. In his will, dated 1829, Erb left money for the use of schools; the interest was to be used 'for the benefit and education of the poor and needy children.' After 1842 the little building was moved to Kitchener and inhabited for nearly fifty years by the family of Levi Carroll. In 1893 it was moved again, this time back to Waterloo, where it is now situated in Waterloo Park near Laurel Creek, one of the tributaries of the Grand River.

The City of Waterloo's identity and reputation have been connected with universities, and it is now also known for high-tech industries. Furthermore, the whole Regional Municipality of Waterloo, which includes Kitchener, Cambridge, and surrounding areas, is a leader in Canada in the conservation of significant natural heritage, and scientists at the University of Waterloo are part of that project. It could be said, therefore, that the scientific work being done on the preservation and restoration of the watershed's environment is—symbolically, at least—part of the heritage of Abraham Erb and his school.

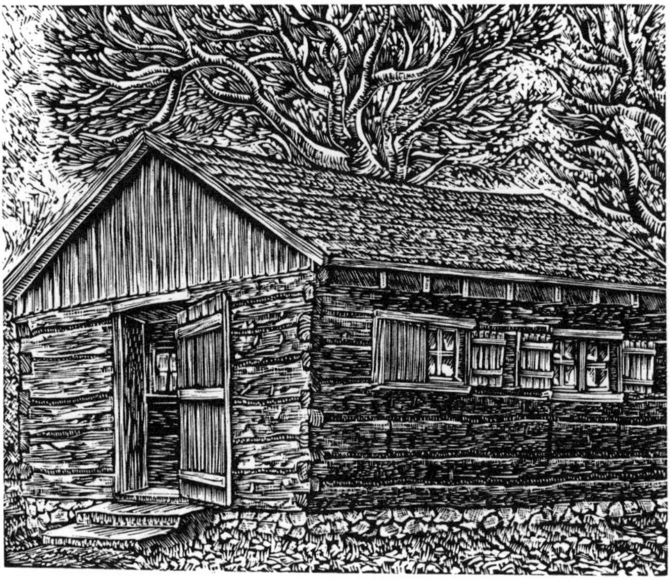

First Waterloo Schoolhouse

Kitchener was founded by a group of Mennonites but soon also attracted immigrants directly from Germany, and it was they who named the settlement Berlin. In their history of the city, John English and Kenneth McLaughlin comment that, while early Mennonites tended not to create villages, the Germans—among whom were many artisans, tradesmen, and industrialists—did. Because Berlin, situated some distance away from the river, had little water power, early industries were steam-powered. Both the German and the industrial elements continue to be important.

This was the setting for the boyhood of William Lyon Mackenzie King (1874–1950), who became Canada's tenth and longest-serving prime minister. He was born in a house on Benton Street but the family moved several times before settling at Woodside when Willie was eleven. He lived there until he enrolled at the University of Toronto. Towards the end of his life he wrote that the years at Woodside 'left the most abiding of all impressions and most in the way of family associations.' He had trees from Woodside transplanted to his Kingsmere estate in the Gatineau hills.

I've noted that he enjoyed fishing in the Grand (see p. 76), but the imprint on him of the Grand River area would have gone beyond that. Growing up in Kitchener, a town with much industry, meant living among people with cultures different from his own Scottish one. This contact with ethnic and working-class issues would have contributed to the understanding that he later brought to his work as an industrial consultant; he became one of the earliest expert practitioners in the emerging field of industrial relations. As prime minister he introduced measures such as unemployment insurance and family allowances.

There is another much less direct connection between King and the Grand: his grandfather William Lyon Mackenzie had from 1851 to 1858 been the member of the legislature for Haldimand County, at the mouth of the river.

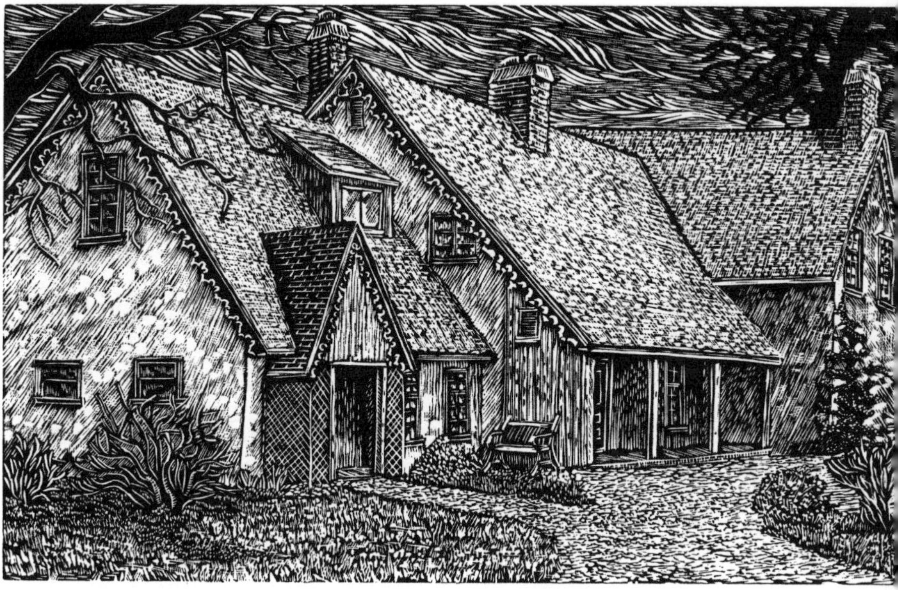

Twilight at Woodside

In the middle of the nineteenth century, Doon was a major milling centre. Besides a flour mill and a cooperage, there was a linen mill making rope, twine, and upholstering material. This mill and its branch in Conestogo employed a hundred people. Other establishments included two churches, a hotel, a school, and a station on the Grand Trunk Railway.

One of the mills, a saw- and woollen mill, belonged to Ransford Watson, father of the landscape painter Homer Watson (1855–1936), an important and widely respected figure in the development of Canadian art. He was born a few yards from the spot from which this view is taken. Because his father was the owner of a water-powered mill, Watson had an intimate and deeply rooted connection with the Grand. After living elsewhere for short spells, he returned to Doon and bought a house, very close to the river, which was his permanent home for the rest of his life and is now the Homer Watson House and Gallery. For a time it was the site of the Doon School of Art, where Carl Schaefer (see p. 30) was an instructor and where Gerard studied in the early 1960s. Among Homer Watson's work are many paintings of the Grand River; Gerard, in this engraving, suggests the kind of view that Watson loved and often depicted.

The structure on the skyline is the Doon Pioneer Tower, built by the Waterloo County Pioneers' Memorial Association as a tribute to the early Mennonite settlers in the area.

In 1893, Watson said that the Grand River valley was 'his heart's home', and, as we've seen, he took an active part in protecting some of the woods that he painted (see p. 16).

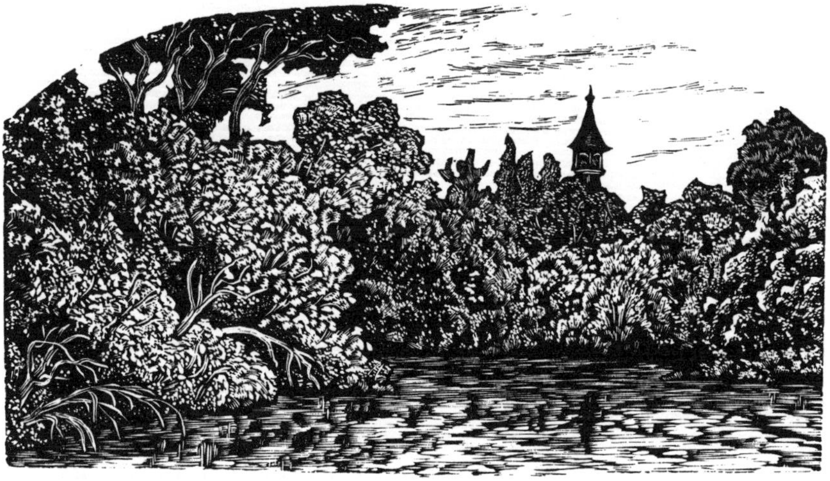

Grand River at Doon

The first settlers in the area of Blair, now part of Cambridge, arrived in 1800, and the development of the village began in 1817. Pioneers built mills, a hotel, and a shingle-roofed covered bridge. Several historic houses still exist.

Of the surviving buildings, the most unusual is the Sheave Tower, connected at one time to the mill across the road whose lower section is still operating as the Blair Flour Mill. Established in 1846, it is the oldest independent family-operated corn mill in Canada.

The Sheave Tower was built about 1876 on Blair Creek (also called Bowman Creek), just above its junction with the Grand River. The creek's water, which would already have turned the wheel at the flour mill, was then channelled to the tower, where it dropped down a well-like structure containing a turbine, rather like a big corkscrew. The turbine's vertical shaft ran up to the top of the tower, where it turned a large sprocket wheel mounted on a horizontal axle that protruded from the tower. The axle is just visible at top right in the engraving. A pulley (or sheave), now missing, engaged a cable that ran to the mill, seventy-three metres away, where it provided extra power at peak periods. This is a remarkable and innovative method for transferring power, and the tower may be the only example of the technology still extant. It was restored in 1998–2000 by Heritage Cambridge and the Waterloo Regional Heritage Foundation.

On the November day when we were there, Gerard waded through undergrowth to find a good angle from which to sketch the tower. A few minutes later I could see him sitting on his shooting stick, drawing. I walked around, feeling my way into the layout of the site and noticing where the tower's dam still is and where the mill's dam must have been. The small road was very quiet. On that day, in that place, time telescoped.

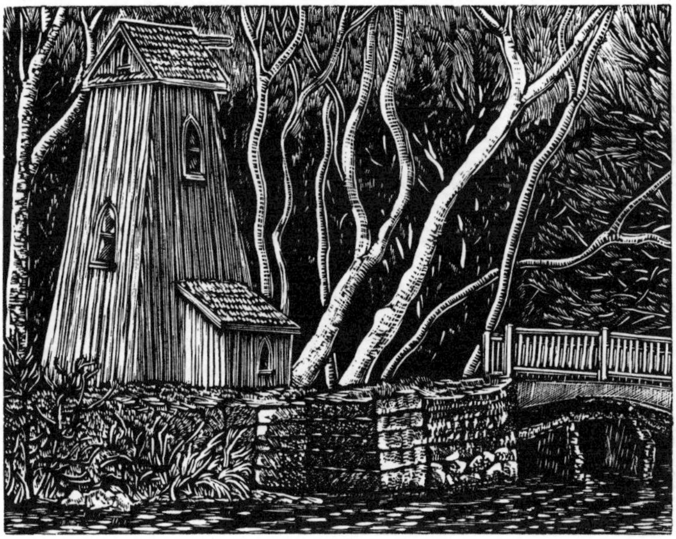

Sheave Tower, Blair

In Cambridge, river and city are tightly melded. The old part of Galt, which is the largest component of the modern merger with Preston and Hespeler that produced Cambridge, hugs the river, but dikes built in the 1980s protect it from floods. Along this stretch there was a dense industrial complex, consisting mainly of foundries and manufacturers of food and clothing. Several buildings have been repurposed, such as the Riverside Silk Mill's conversion into the University of Waterloo's School of Architecture. Those that survive represent a century—from the 1840s to the 1930s—of Canadian manufacturing.

Galt's industrial character was established by Absalom Shade. Beginning in 1816, he worked with William Dickson (see p. 24), who had bought the land from the Six Nations. Shade built a bridge and refurbished a derelict gristmill, then built a new gristmill as well as a distillery. He constructed roads and opened a store. From the Canada Company he received large contracts to supply lumber, flour, pork, and other provisions. He supported the Grand River Navigation Company, having experimented with shipping flour down the river on barges until one of the vessels was destroyed in a flood.

Gerard and I went down to water level so that he could make a sketch (for a different engraving than the one given here). The protective walls suggested to us the Seine where it passes through Paris. The river was low, with bouldery banks on both sides, and there was a brisk current. Ducks swam by and gulls winged past. In spite of the city buildings visible above the walls, the river was living its private life.

The image shows a bowstring bridge, one of a number built in the watershed in the late 1920s and early 1930s. The design may have been brought to the area by Charles (Carlo) Mattaini, a bridge builder who came here from northern Italy, where such bridges are common.

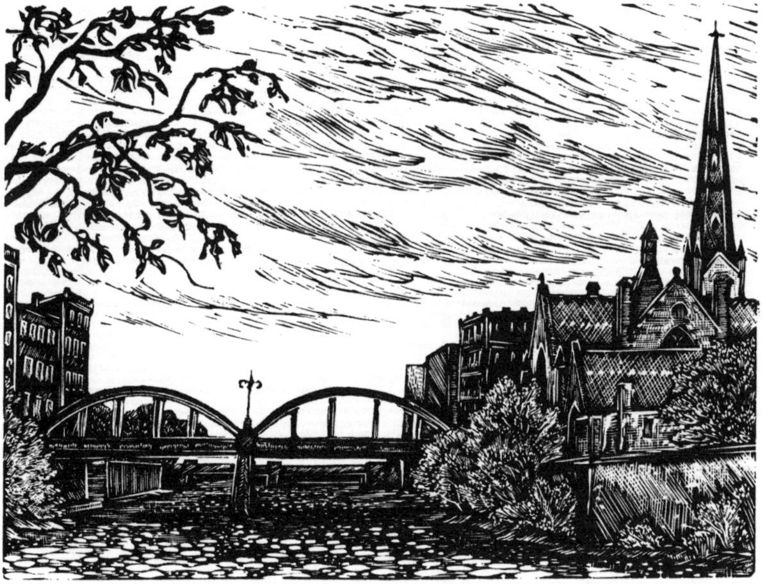

Grand River at Galt

This ruined mill is an exceptionally impressive building. The walls are nearly a metre thick and in places still stand three storeys high. As the engraving shows, they are beautifully crafted, with attention paid to style as well as function and durability. All this is clearly visible because, with the roof missing, the interior is well lit. It is about twelve by eighteen metres. It has the dignity and even the grandeur of ruined castles in Europe.

Ruins are important. At the most immediate level they are picturesque elements of landscape but, more significantly, they give us a strong sense of the layers of history. That awareness gives perspective to the present, adds the dimension of depth.

Information about the mill is full of inconsistencies but sources do agree that it was constructed by the brothers Alva and Sydney German in about 1870 as a woollen mill. The works were powered by water from the river, channelled under the building via the arch shown here; the mill race is also still visible. After the woollen-milling operation closed, the building became a hotel called the Grand River Lodge. It had reception rooms on the ground floor and thirteen bedrooms upstairs. J.M. Merriman, writing for the Brantford *Expositor*, saw the interior in 1944 when it was abandoned but still contained all its fittings and even a grand piano in one of the two dining rooms.

Demolition has been threatened several times, but for the moment the building still stands. Members of Hamilton Paranormal report that it is haunted.

One of our visits was on an autumn day. The fall colours and the subdued murmur of the river flowing only yards away from the building created a mood of nostalgia.

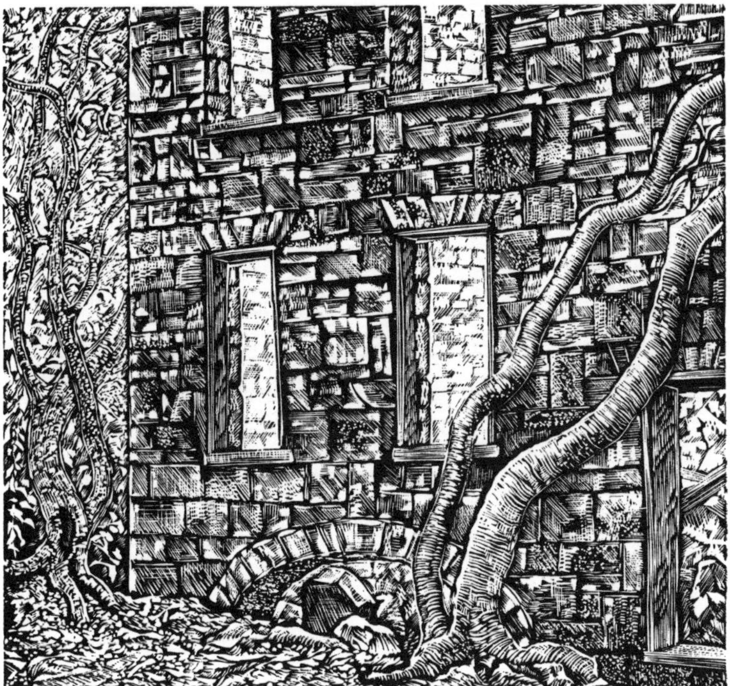

Ruins of German's Mill near Glen Morris

The beauty of the river is abundantly evident here. Its curving course is pleasing to the eye, and so are the wooded banks. This is just upstream from Paris; Gerard and I are sitting on a bluff on a mild November afternoon, looking southwest so that the sun is in our eyes and reflects off the surface of the water.

We are seeing the river as it would have been seen by First Peoples and early settlers. Hiram Capron, the founder of Paris, wrote to his brother: 'The river here, too, flows in graceful curves and, divided by pleasant islands, is lost to the eye among the lovely woodlands.'

This part of the river is particularly popular with walkers and canoeists. The Cambridge-to-Paris trail runs along it, following the roadbed of the former Lake Erie and Northern Railway, one of the last electric railways built in Ontario.

It is also ecologically significant because this is the Carolinian life zone. The stretch of the Grand from Cambridge to Paris contains some relatively undisturbed old-growth forest, especially close to the banks of the river. On this November day the trees are bare, but on another of our trips, made in June, we drove along the other bank and saw how lush the vegetation is. It was hard to put myself in the mind of a settler lifting his axe to demolish such beauty; I understand the necessity that drove him, but still it was a disturbing idea.

Gerard observed that here we could see the river in its natural grandeur, see clearly how it has sculpted its course and written itself on the landscape, and hear the dialogue of land and water. As in the Elora Gorge, the view here is a lesson in geology and in how rivers create landscape.

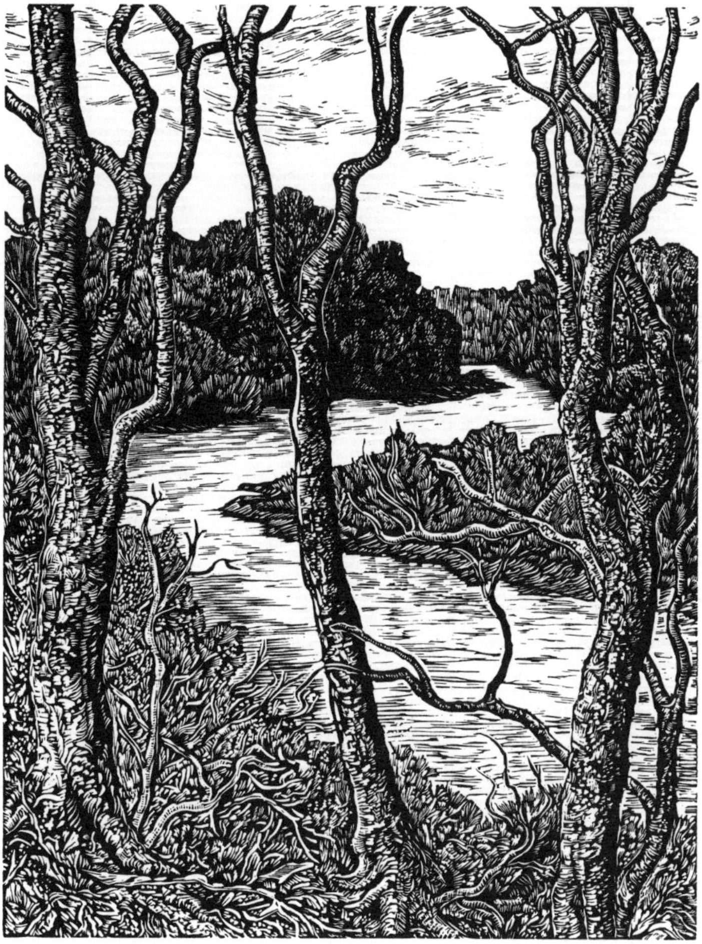

A Shining Ribbon of Water

Paris was built around this very spot, where the Grand River is joined by one of its main tributaries, the Nith. The first settler, an Englishman named William Holme, arrived in 1821, intending to establish a large estate for himself. It was he who began mining gypsum in the area and set up a small grinding mill powered by the Nith. In 1829 he sold his property to Hiram Capron, an American, who laid out the town plot and enlarged both mine and mill, and who is credited with being the town's founder.

Gypsum, or plaster of Paris (the origin of the town's name), was used for fertilizer and as a building material, and later as a component in paint. Holme's mine and mill were the first in Ontario. Later, more would be opened in the area, and the gypsum was moved on scows downriver and through the Grand River Navigation canal system.

Other industries also used the river's current for power: Paris was for decades the headquarters of Penmans, the manufacturer of underwear, hosiery, sweaters, and blankets. In 1868 the firm, which was a woollen factory and carding mill, had moved here from Woodstock and occupied a converted sawmill at the junction of the Nith and the Grand. By 1890 it was the largest supplier of such goods in Canada. The Paris plant operated until 1981.

The water-powered mills that once functioned all along the Grand have now either vanished, or they are ruins, or they have been repurposed. Penmans, however, continued beyond the pioneer period and the era of early industrialization. What has survived is not the physical building but the company, which became a major industry. But both strands—the firm, in this case, and the building in other instances—have their roots in the typical water-powered riverside mill serving the needs of settlers.

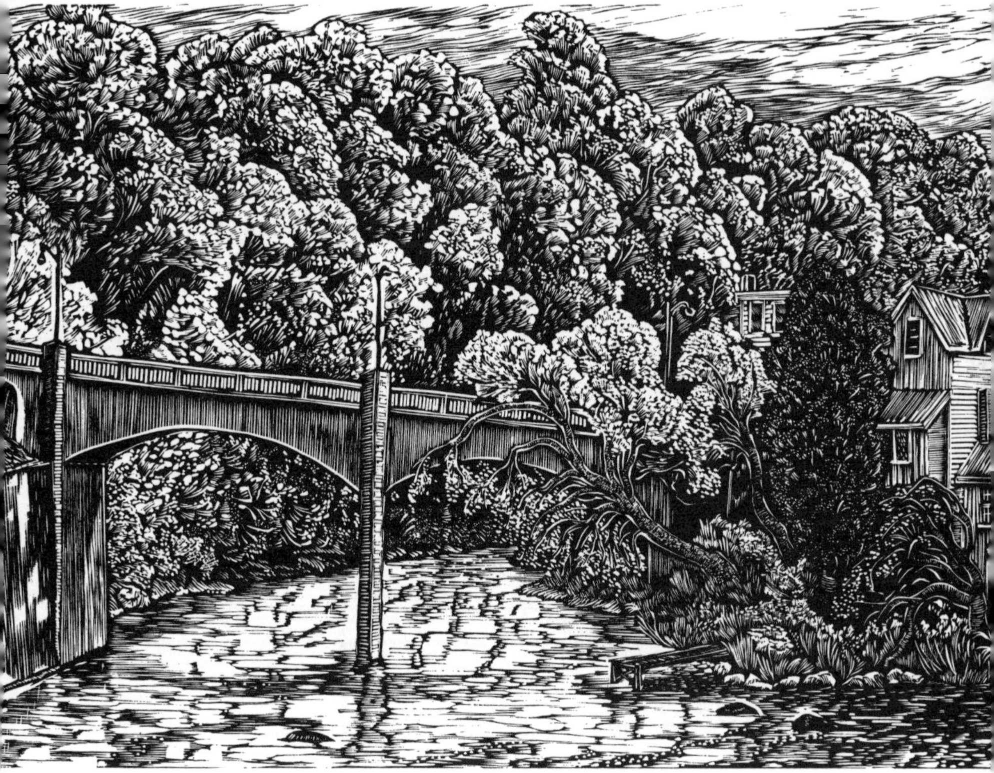

The Junction of the Nith and Grand Rivers at Paris

Paris is known for its cobblestone buildings, buildings that are finished in the kind of facing shown in the engraving. The technique was brought here in the late 1830s by Levi Boughton, a mason from New York State, and was used until the middle of the 1860s, at which time brick became more common. Thirteen buildings in the Paris area feature this kind of construction. The house in the image—the Scott House at 2 Arnold Street, dating from the 1840s—has cobblestone facing on its foundation; the rest of the building has stucco.

The cobbles for these buildings, collected locally in fields and along the river, would have been shaped and smoothed either by glaciers or by the water of the river. This means that there is an intimate connection between these structures and the Grand; looking at a cobblestone wall, you can almost hear the voice of the river.

Paris is at the northern end of the stretch of the Grand that has been designated 'Exceptional Waters'. This section is considered exceptional because it is a good habitat for a wide range of fish species, because much of it is bounded by a fringe of virtually untouched Carolinian forest, and because this stretch was historically important for transportation, gypsum mining, and water power.

Part of the concept behind the 'Exceptional Waters' designation is that a reach of river so labelled can be used as a centre of excellence, an example and a standard for the rest of the watershed.

The resources are managed by local communities, anglers' and naturalists' associations, and many similar groups. The work is supported by governments and foundations, and by the Grand River Conservation Authority, the University of Guelph, the Six Nations of the Grand River, and others—a many-sided partnership.

But the principal partner is the river itself.

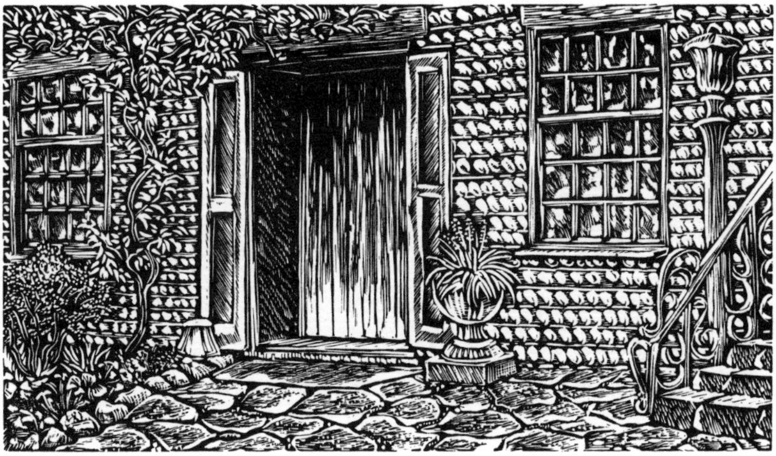

Cobblestone Dooryard, Paris

The area around Whiteman's Creek has, like other parts of the valley, been occupied by humans since shortly after the retreat of the glaciers. Nomadic Paleo-Indians hunted and camped here, and a significant archaeological site dates from AD 1350–1450. The Neutrals (the Attiwandaron) living in this region in the seventeenth century were visited by European missionaries. An important and probably ancient trail stretching from Lake Ontario to the Detroit area crossed the Grand here and was still in use in 1793 when Lieutenant Governor John Graves Simcoe travelled this way.

When the Six Nations moved into the lower Grand River valley in 1784, the family of Chief David Hill settled at this location. For First Peoples, river confluences are sacred, and there's evidence that this junction was such a place.

In the 1830s that village was ravaged by cholera and apparently more or less abandoned. Following its demise, European settlers came to the area, including several retired army and navy men. One of them, Major Arnold Robinson Burrowes, bought an extensive tract of land and in 1840, on the north side of the creek, he built a large house called Strathmore Farm. He raised Shorthorn cattle and also bred fine horses and had a racetrack. He constructed a dam on the creek and used the water power to operate a plaster mill, a sawmill, a flour mill, and a distillery. A footbridge connected the two banks of the creek. It is said that up to eighteen families lived nearby and worked in Burrowes's various operations.

The area is now the site of the Francis Sandy Theological Centre for Native Peoples, and of the Five Oaks Education and Retreat Centre of The United Church of Canada. Interestingly, that completes the circle back to the original Native Peoples' use of the area as a site of religious significance. The Hill family's house stood on the retreat centre's property until it was demolished in the 1960s.

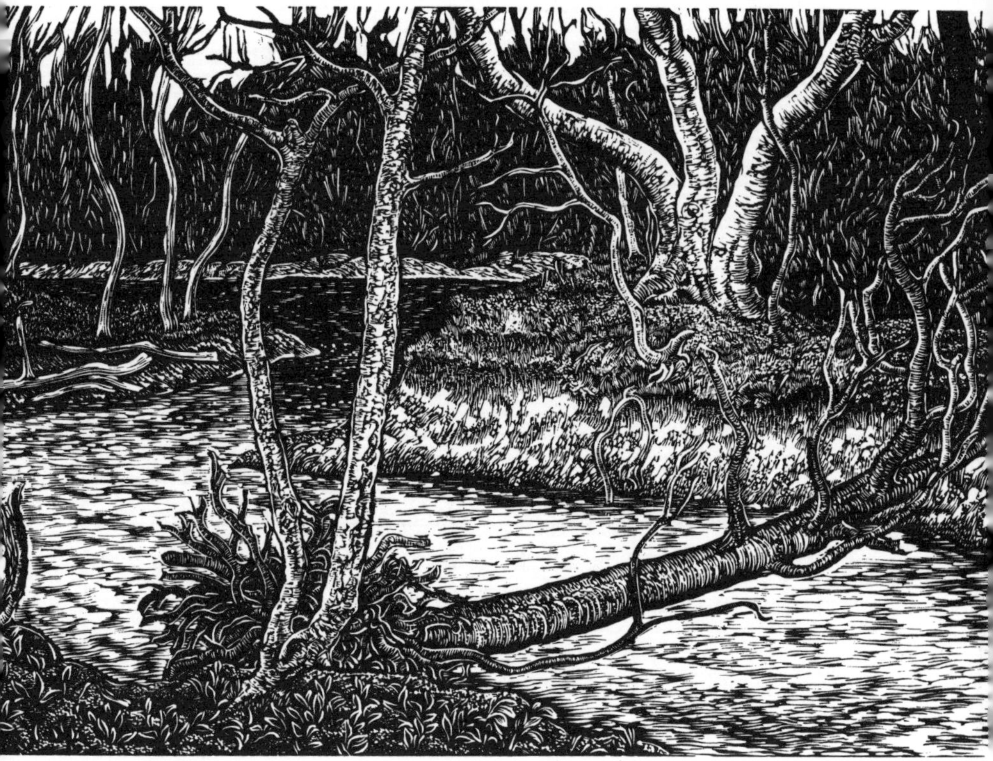

The Junction of Whiteman's Creek and the Grand River

The Brantford area is rich in early Aboriginal history. The valley of the Grand supplied a profusion of the natural resources that the First Peoples needed, and the region seems to have been continuously used and occupied from about AD 600–800 to the middle of the seventeenth century.

One of the settlements is what is now known as the Walker site, an Attiwandaron village east of Brantford and close to the river, which was excavated, designated as a National Historic Site, and then covered again. It was occupied during the 1630s and 1640s and was, in 1640–41, visited by the Jesuits Brébeuf and Chaumonot (see p. 9).

In that early period, villages would be moved every few decades as buildings deteriorated or the local resources were exhausted. One of the resources whose depletion impelled these moves was soil. By the sixteenth century the Iroquois way of life was based on agriculture, and that enabled them to form sizeable villages. The main food crops were corn, beans, and squash, called the Three Sisters, and many varieties of each were grown. As shown in the engraving, the corn was planted in small mounds of soil; when the stalks began to grow, they supported the vines of the beans planted around them. Squash was grown among the mounds and, besides producing food, helped to control weeds. Tobacco, used for ritual purposes, was also extensively cultivated.

The Three Sisters, which provided a balanced diet, were supplemented by roots, berries, greens, nuts, fish, and meat from the wild.

Settlement continued in the Brantford area after the granting of the land to the Six Nations. It was on a bluff overlooking the river that Joseph Brant established the Mohawk Village; Davisville (see p. 11) was nearby.

Like the Three Sisters, this long history of human occupation had its roots in the soil of the valley that the river created.

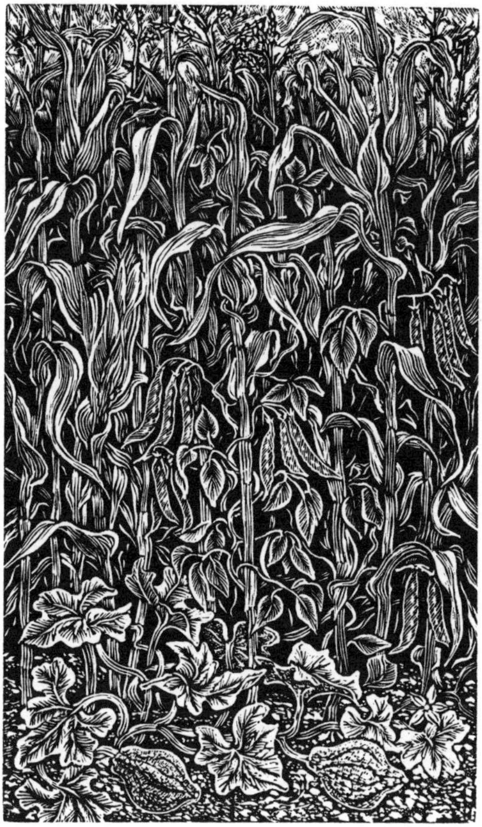

The Three Sisters

The Time Office, and the entrance portico of the office building that, until recently, adjoined it, are all that remain of the enormous Cockshutt Plow Company, founded in 1877. They are now backed by brownfield. This little building was constructed in 1903, with the façade added in 1912. Although it's a functional structure, the architect made it interesting by ornamenting it with neo-Romanesque details. Both it and the office building were described in a 2012 Heritage Impact Assessment study as 'historically and architecturally significant'.

Beyond the brownfield is the Grand River Navigation's canal. After its opening in 1848, this section of canal, which included a dam and three locks, contributed significantly to Brantford's becoming an industrial centre. Though the railway reached Brantford in 1854 and the canal company went bankrupt in 1861, the canal continued carrying traffic for a couple of decades longer. The dam provided hydro-electric power for industries near the locks and also for the town.

In the later nineteenth and early twentieth centuries, Brantford was a major industrial city. It was especially famous for agricultural machinery: equipment built by the Cockshutt Plow Company was exported worldwide and was important in the opening of the Canadian West. But when, in the 1960s and '70s, the local industrial sector declined sharply, the very size of the industrial building stock was a problem. Buildings that were landmarks in Canada's industrial heritage were left empty and eventually demolished. The Cockshutt office building was badly damaged by fire in March 2012 and then, along with several other structures from the same era, was taken down by order of the city council—except for the portico. Important heritage buildings in the city centre were also demolished, but recently a number of others have been saved and repurposed for Wilfrid Laurier University's Brantford campus.

There are plans to restore the Time Office and make it the centrepiece of an industrial heritage park.

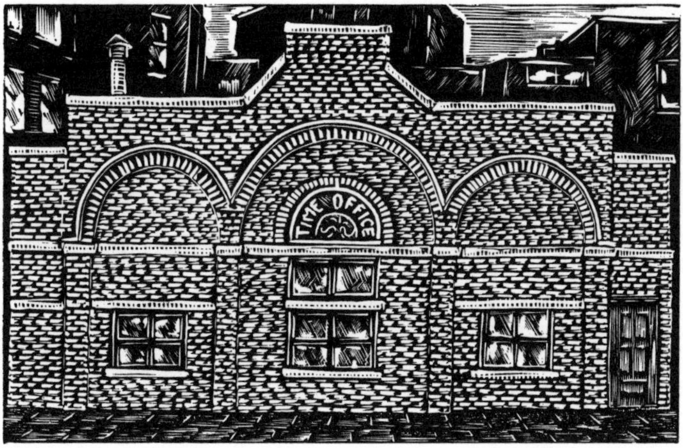

Time Office, Cockshutt Plow Company, Brantford

There is an evocative word-picture of Alexander Graham Bell (1847–1922) sitting on a height of land behind this house—the Bell family home near Brantford—gazing over the Grand River. Here, in what he called his 'dreaming place', he had, on 26 July 1874, the inspiration for the breakthrough that made the telephone possible.

He was twenty-three in 1870 when the family moved from Scotland to this property in Brantford, now the Bell Homestead National Historic Site. They were part of the post-pioneer migration to the Grand River valley. Though they farmed on a small scale, they were professional people. Alexander Melville Bell, A. G.'s father, lectured on philology in Kingston and Boston, and in 1881 he and his wife moved to Washington, D.C., where he worked in education of the deaf.

Alexander Graham Bell had moved to Boston in 1871 but while his parents still lived in Brantford he regularly visited them; later he would say that the telephone was conceived in Brantford and born in Boston. While best known for inventing the telephone, teaching the deaf, and experimenting with flight, his interests ranged much further. He was the second president of the National Geographic Society. He did pioneering work with X-ray technology and with inventions that led to the iron lung and ultrasound. He held patents for phonographic inventions. He built hydrofoils. He was interested in music and photography. In a 1917 paper on the depletion of natural resources, he wrote that the unchecked burning of fossil fuels would lead to a 'sort of greenhouse effect' and global warming.

Though only a short part of his life was spent in southern Ontario, Bell is connected with the Grand River because the first two of his longer telephone calls were made between Brantford and Mount Pleasant (six and a half kilometres away) and between Brantford and Paris, Ontario. George Johnson, Pauline Johnson's father, was present on the latter occasion.

Like the watershed's, Bell's work is all about connections.

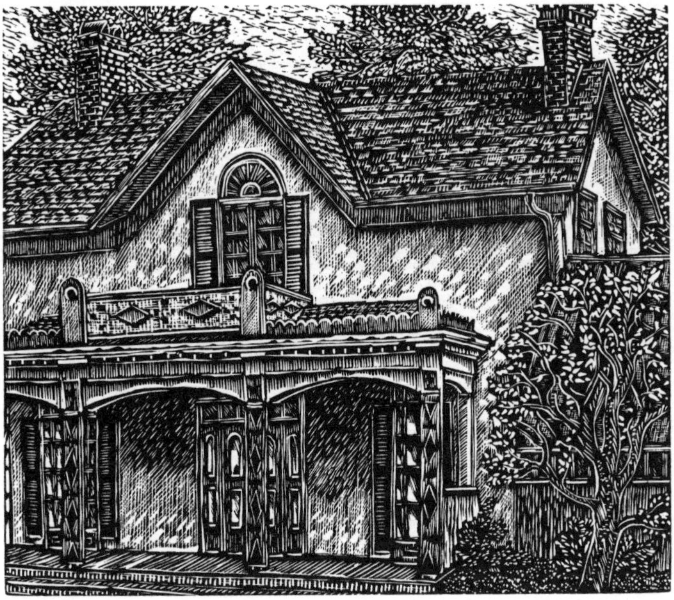

Bell Homestead, Brantford

This is the Grand River as it flows through the Six Nations Reserve. The river was the central feature in the strip of land (consisting of ten kilometres along each bank) that Sir Frederick Haldimand, governor of Quebec (see p. 10), granted to the Six Nations who had remained loyal to the British during the American War of Independence. About 1,800 members of the Six Nations Confederacy settled along the river in separate but linked villages; the Mohawk Village was the largest.

As recounted in the introduction, Joseph Brant's gifts and sale of extensive tracts of this territory to European land speculators led to years of disputes between the Six Nations and the British government and its colonial representatives. But even the territory that was left after these transactions were finalized was not to remain entirely in the hands of the Six Nations. In 1841, a reserve was established, about 190 square kilometres in extent. Members of the Six Nations who lived in villages outside the Reserve could move to it if they wished.

In 1847, an area in the southwest corner of the reserve was transferred to the Mississaugas, who had had to leave their land on the Credit River near Toronto because of encroachment by European settlers.

About 50 percent of the reserve is covered by Carolinian forest—a higher proportion for such an area than is found in any other part of the watershed, and the largest single block of Carolinian woodland in Canada. The Six Nations are active in matters of wildlife and water management, and other environmental issues, sitting on many committees concerned with everything from fish ladders to ecosystem restoration, from spills notification to archaeology. There is an agreement in place—negotiated in 1996 and the first of its kind in Canada—that allows such participation without prejudicing outstanding land claims.

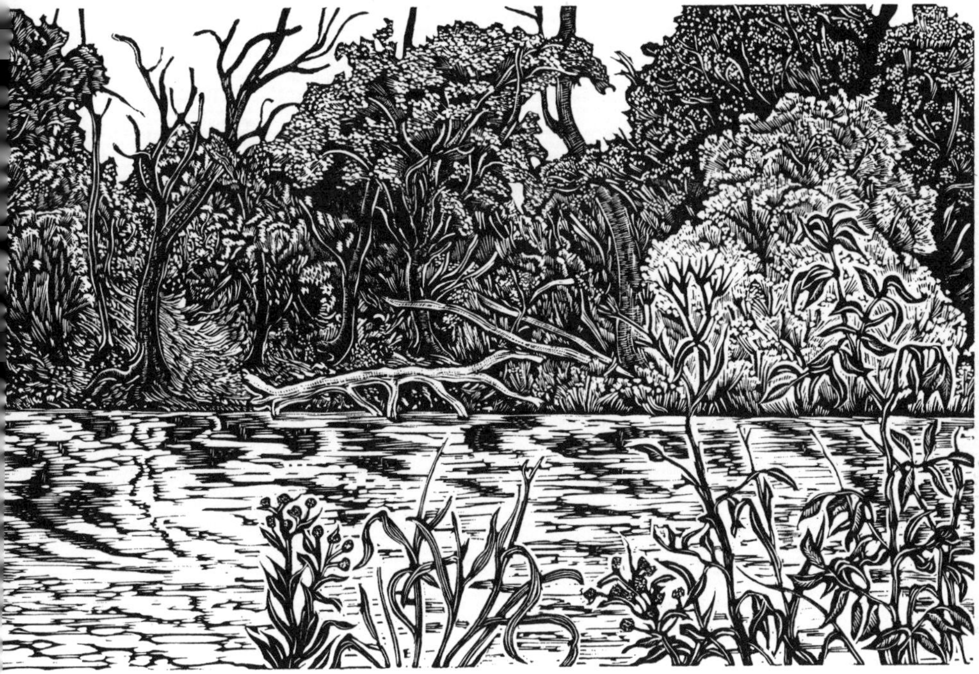

The Grand River at Six Nations Reserve

Chiefswood is where Pauline Johnson was born and where she lived until, at age twenty-three, she moved to Brantford with her sister and widowed mother. It is a Regency villa, and its two identical fronts symbolize the fact that the Johnson family was a merging of Mohawk and English cultures. At the same time it is a house of its place and time. The walls are of walnut and were built using plank-on-plank construction, a technique only possible in an area where timber was abundant.

By some sleight of hand, the interior seems far larger than is suggested by the exterior. Standing in the house now, it is easy to imagine it fully furnished and inhabited, serving as an elegant setting for the Johnsons' frequent entertaining. In 1869 Prince Arthur, later Duke of Connaught and Strathearn, was here in connection with his investiture as a Chief of the Six Nations. Two Governors General and their wives visited: Lord and Lady Dufferin in 1874, and the Marquess of Lorne and Princess Louise in 1879. So did the artist Homer Watson, the world-famous anthropologist Horatio Hale, and the inventor Alexander Graham Bell. From them Pauline, who in her performing years would show herself to be a skilful mimic, learned the ways and the conversation that would later make her welcome in the drawing-rooms of the English aristocracy as well as in those of leaders of Canadian society.

Chiefswood is on the bank of the river, and the Johnson children learned early to paddle a canoe. With Pauline, canoeing became a passion. She was very adept, and during her years at Chiefswood and in Brantford it was to the river that she turned for comfort and a refreshing of her spirits. She frequently wrote about it; her most famous poem is 'The Song My Paddle Sings'.

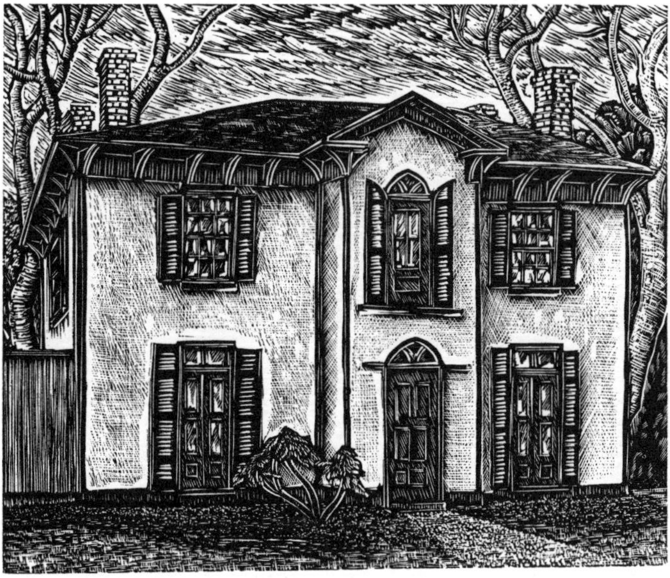

Chiefswood, Home of Pauline Johnson

Middleport, now very small, has a multi-layered past. First Peoples villages existed here at various periods between AD 1000 and European contact. After 1784, the Onondagas and Tuscaroras settled in this area. Since the forming of the Iroquois Confederacy, the Onondagas had been the keepers of the great council fire; now, therefore, the council house was established in the Onondaga Village on what became the western edge of Middleport. The council met here until 1856, when the Indian Superintendent forced it to move to Ohsweken, on the reserve.

European Middleport was founded by John Solomon Hagar in November 1838. The local Iroquois, for whom some of the land was sacred, attempted to drive him off but after a violent confrontation the controversy went to court and Hagar won.

The village, a port on the canal system, derived its name from its position halfway between Caledonia and the locks at Brantford. Like other riverside villages, it served a hinterland of farms and hamlets. These villages were channels through which people, merchandise, and the products of local industries flowed. A settlement of a couple of hundred residents sounds tiny to us but its services and facilities would make it a centre for miles of surrounding countryside. General stores were vital to this system, selling items that could not be made at home, providing credit, and serving as outposts of the empire-wide commercial network centred in Britain. The store depicted in the engraving is one of the surviving early buildings in Middleport. Like Chiefswood, it was built using plank-on-plank construction.

Middleport dwindled with the depletion of the forests on which its logging industry depended, and with the decline of the canal system. But in 1883 it still contained two general stores, two blacksmith shops, a wagon and carriage shop, a bakery, a hotel, two churches, and a post office. Just behind the town was a station on the Grand Trunk Railway, and for years there was a ferry across the river here.

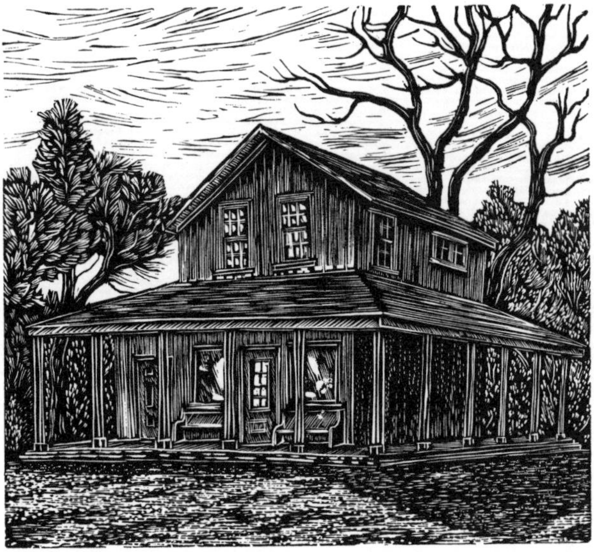

General Store, Middleport

The Carolinian zone in southern Ontario is characterized by plants and animals that are associated with areas far to the south of here. Both the opossum and the southern flying squirrel are now found in Canada. So are trees such as the tulip tree, sassafras, flowering dogwood, pawpaw, and sycamore. Black walnut is an indicator tree for the zone but the area also includes sugar maple, beech, oak, basswood, and ash.

As mentioned in the introduction, this life zone is seriously threatened. The work of protecting what is left, and of regeneration and replacement, is carried on by many organizations, private and public. Stewardship programs involving local landowners are particularly important; this approach, pioneered here, has now been adopted elsewhere in Canada. Conservation science is also contributing, stressing the fact that 'islands of green' need to be large enough and that, in order for them and their wildlife populations to survive, they need to be connected by corridors.

The Carolinian zone is of particular interest at this time because, with the climate changing, these plant and animal species are likely to move northwards. Global warming has already, in the past hundred years, allowed birds such as cardinals and mourning doves to extend their breeding range into southern Ontario.

The green dragon, pictured in this image, is a rare plant that is another of the indicator species for the Carolinian life zone. It is a close relative of the jack-in-the-pulpit and likes rich flood-plain woods. We found it in a forest where there was moist soil and dappled sunlight. On that humid, thundery day in a swampy area close to a brimful stream, it was easy to feel that we were in a far more southern climate.

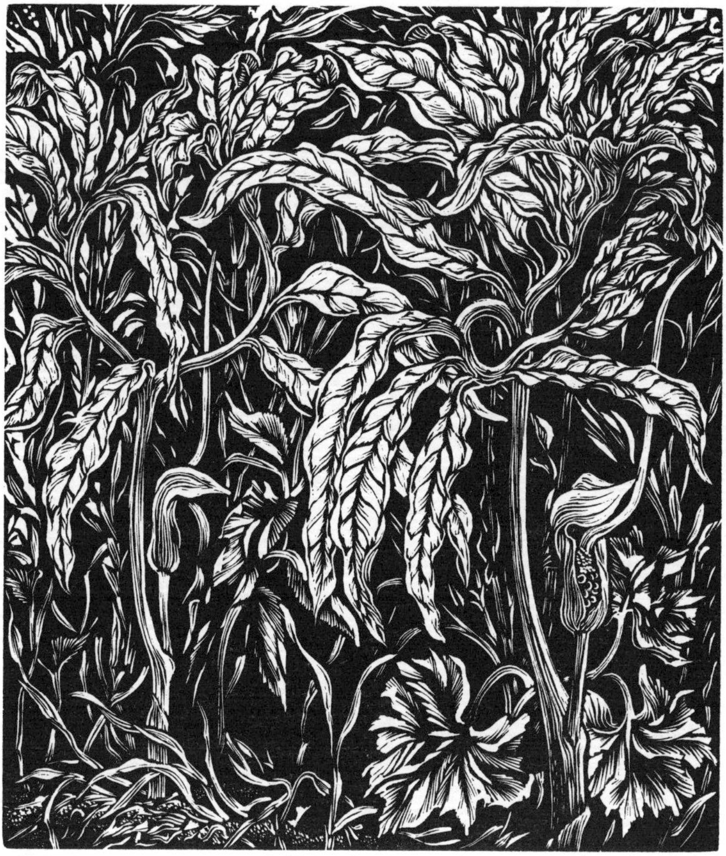

Green Dragon

This is the only mill remaining of the many that once existed in Caledonia. It was a gristmill, built around 1853, water-powered like almost all the early mills and continuing to be so until the end of its mill life in the early 1960s. The flour was sent beyond the immediate area, perhaps at first on the canal system and then by the railway, which reached Caledonia in 1852. Planning is taking place for adaptive reuse of the building.

Gypsum mining and milling have also, for more than a century, been important in Caledonia's story, and gypsum milling continued to be so until the plant that manufactured gypsum wallboard was idled in early 2014. Until 2004 it had been using gypsum mined along the lower Grand. Gypsum is part of the geology of the Grand River valley, and it would be interesting to know how many houses in Ontario and elsewhere have Grand River gypsum in their construction, and how many acres of agricultural land were fertilized with it.

If mills were crucial to the settlement of Canada, so were canoes. The stretch of the river from Caledonia to Cayuga is now, every summer, the site of the Day of 1,000 Canoes. The festival, which brings together people of the Six Nations and those of European descent, is a reminder of the canoe's importance in Canada's history and of the fact that it was used both by the First Peoples and by the European explorers and fur traders. The Canadian Heritage Rivers System—of which the Grand is a part—chose the canoe as its logo to represent Canada's history and especially the enormously significant role that rivers play in Canada's geography and identity.

The river, here, is crossed by a nine-span bowstring bridge, built in 1917, the only such bridge of this size in Canada. It is slated for demolition, and its disappearance will be a major loss.

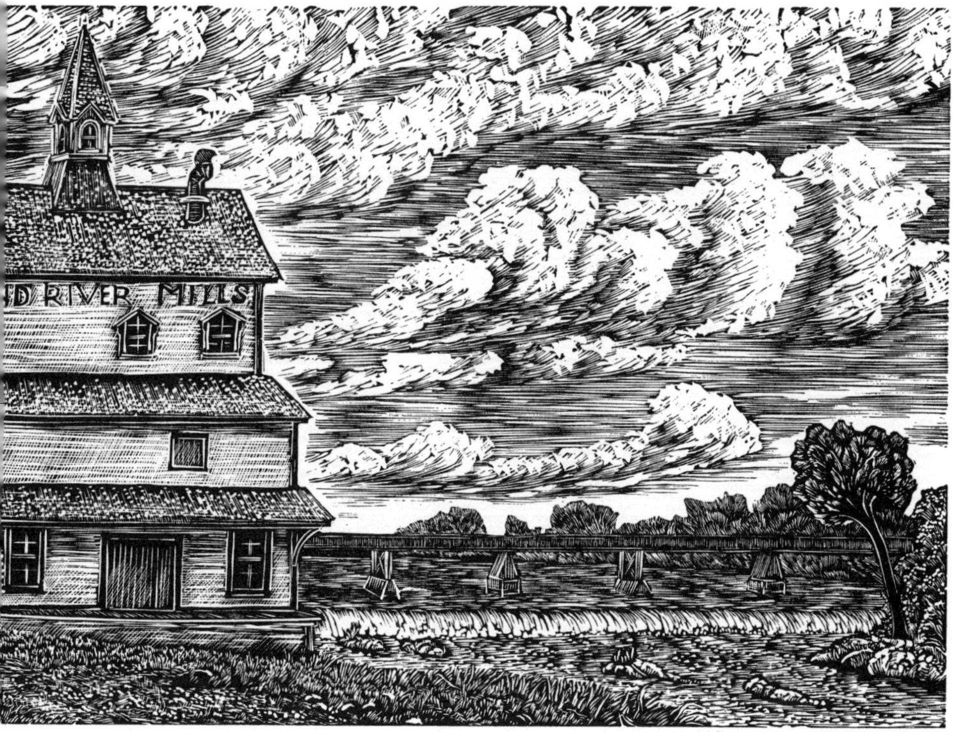

Grand River Mills, Caledonia

What is now the small village of York was first named the Nelles Settlement, after the family that settled here. The Nelles family, which was of German origin, had lived close to the Six Nations along the Mohawk River in what is now New York State. During the American War of Independence they fought by the side of the Six Nations and other loyalists; when the Six Nations received land along the Grand River, Joseph Brant gave an extensive tract to Hendrick Nelles. In 1796 Hendrick built a house that is still standing and still occupied by a descendant. The settlement's name was changed to York after the city on the north shore of Lake Ontario became Toronto.

In June of 1834, York came to more vigorous life with the building of the Grand River Navigation Company's canal and lock. Construction workers moved in, and by 1846 there were about 150 inhabitants. It had a gristmill, sawmill, and shingle factory; when Smith's Canadian Gazetteer was being prepared in 1846, all three of these had just burned down but were about to be rebuilt. York also accommodated a physician and a surgeon, three stores, three taverns, two wagon makers, three tailors, two cabinetmakers, four shoemakers, and two churches with resident ministers. Nearby was a gypsum mill to which raw gypsum was brought for grinding.

Because of the river and canal, the life of the town included a wharf and the steamboats, barges, and log rafts moving up and down the river. It was a busy town, very unlike the scene depicted here.

With the decline of the canal system, York also declined, but the drop was not immediate. After the Grand River Navigation Company went bankrupt, the locks and canals continued to operate for some time, and barges were still used for shipping gypsum and similar bulky freight. The railway passed by three kilometres away and York reinvented itself again, recapturing something of its pre-canal serenity.

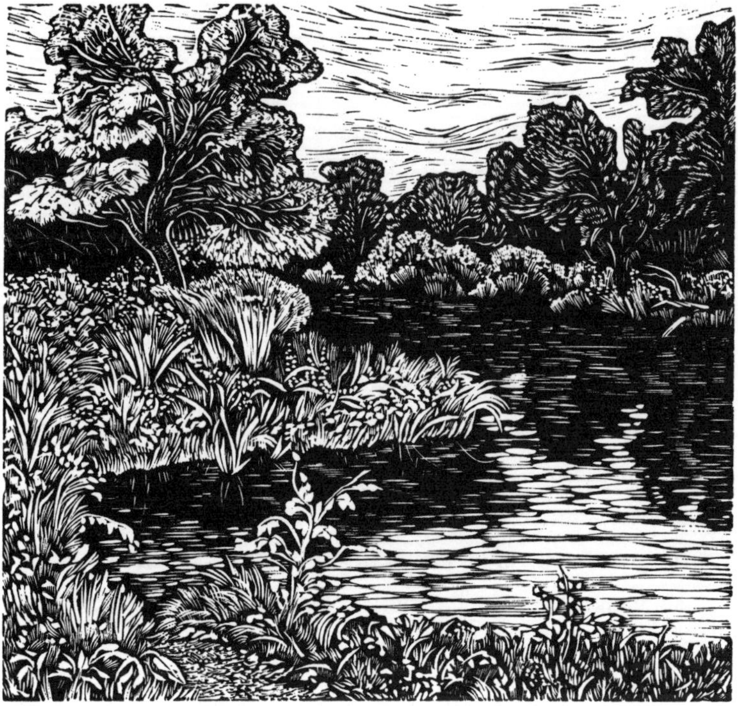

The Grand River at York

The Nelles family, as we've seen, were among the first settlers on the Grand. One of Hendrick's sons was Warner (1771–1846), aged about thirteen when the family arrived here. He became a major landowner in the York area and a supporter of the Grand River Navigation Company.

Another family member prominent in the valley was Warner's nephew Abram Nelles (1805–1863), a Church of England clergyman, missionary, and translator. He began work among the Six Nations in 1827 and became rector of the Mohawk Chapel and principal of the Mohawk Institute, where he taught George Johnson, the future father of Pauline Johnson. Abram Nelles published a book of hymns and psalms in Mohawk and also translated the Book of Common Prayer. He was respected by both the Six Nations and the Europeans and is buried in the chapel's churchyard.

These connections give a glimpse of the social life along this part of the river in the third quarter of the nineteenth century. Warner and Abram Nelles would almost certainly have known all the Six Nations leaders, including George Johnson of Chiefswood. They would have known Peter Jones (see p. 22), the half-Mississauga missionary who had lived among the Six Nations in his youth and was by 1851 in Brantford, and Adam Elliott, the Church of England missionary who lived almost next door to Chiefswood and whose sister-in-law Emily was George Johnson's wife. Johnson and Peter Jones knew each other for thirty years, as Johnson said in a tribute to Jones after the latter's death.

These families would no doubt have met at each other's houses, including the one depicted in the engraving. Besides the fact that Johnson's and Elliott's wives were sisters, it is easy to imagine that Emily Johnson and Eliza Jones (Englishwomen married to First Nations men) would be drawn to each other. All of them were educated people in positions of leadership in the small society along the river from Brantford to York.

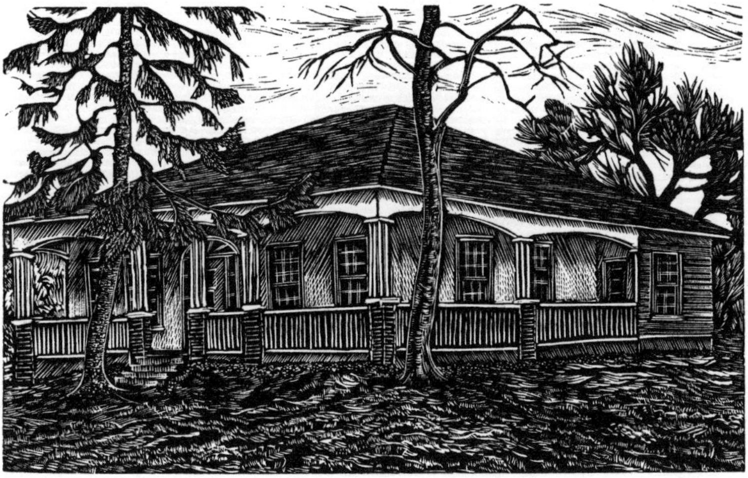

Warner Nelles House, York

The Dochstader Hotel is one of two buildings that survive of Mount Healy (or Healey), a village born of the Grand River Navigation Company's canal. John Donaldson, the village's founder, built a large sawmill and sent the lumber through the canal system to several Great Lakes ports. He also shipped gypsum, which was mined on his land and refined in his mill. And he had a grist mill.

The hotel was built in 1854 by Henry Dochstader, member of another prominent local family, and functioned until 1875. Like the Donaldson mills, it would have been one of the focal points of the village.

We would probably be surprised to realize how many travellers passed through a village like this, and hotels were more important at that time than similar accommodation is nowadays because fewer miles could then be covered in a day. Some travellers would stay with friends, and there might be boarding houses for others, but even quite small villages had hotels. They would be used by commercial travellers, government officials such as surveyors, and settlers heading for their land for the first time. Men working temporarily on local construction projects might also stay there.

And they were indispensable gathering places for the local people, for both formal meetings and casual gatherings, providing some social life during the hard and lonely years of clearing land and getting established. No doubt they were places where information was exchanged, news passed on, labourers hired, tools and livestock bought and sold.

This building is extremely well constructed, the exterior walls being up to four bricks thick; the bricks were made on-site and the interior plaster was produced locally using gypsum from the Donaldson mine. The old riverside road ran between the hotel and the river; the engraving depicts the side that then greeted travellers by both land and water. It must have been a welcome sight.

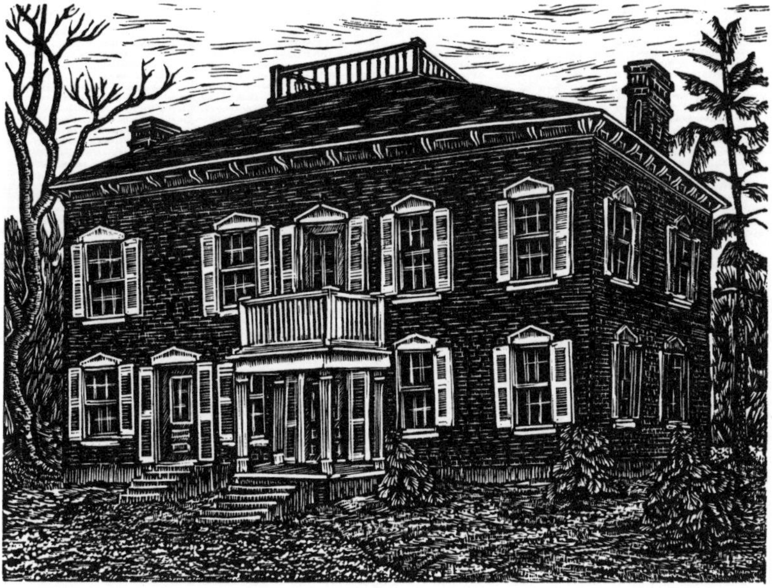

Dochstader Hotel, Mount Healy

Ruthven Park is a stately home, the showplace of a family that became rich during the Canadian version of the Industrial Revolution; anyone who has visited such houses in Europe will recognize the type. Clearly such an image was also in the mind of its builder, David Thompson (1793–1851), who had the building constructed in 1845–47. An advertisement for the gristmill that he owned gives his address as 'Ruthven Mansion'.

Thompson was born and grew up in the Niagara area. After fighting in the War of 1812, he worked as a contractor on the first Welland Canal and became wealthy. He bought land in various locations but settled in this village, called Indiana. He was a major shareholder in and promoter of the Grand River Navigation Company, building a lock at Indiana. He also established two sawmills, a gristmill, a carding mill, a cooperage, and several stores. Other industries in the town included a distillery and a pail factory, and there were two inns. There was also a Black settlement. For some years in the second half of the nineteenth century, Indiana had over thirty industries and was said to be the largest industrial town in Haldimand County.

In 1842 Thompson was elected as the county's first member of the Legislative Assembly of Upper Canada.

The five generations of Thompsons who owned and occupied the house until 1993 would have seen the town dying around them, houses being demolished, the canal system falling into disrepair and disuse. It is hard not to feel the sadness of all that human effort and emotional investment having such an ending.

But it is a story of transmutation and preservation as well. The house and the 607 hectares of land are now a National Historic Site owned and operated by the Lower Grand River Land Trust, which protects them and also the natural features, including 364 hectares of Carolinian forest.

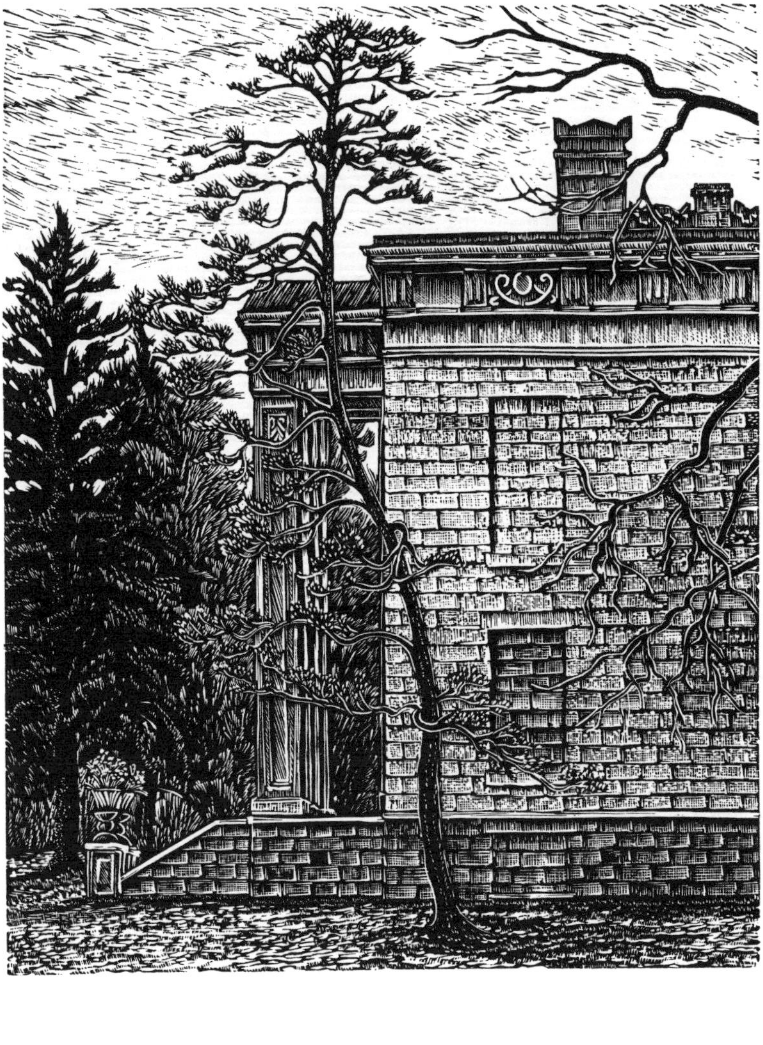

Pine at Ruthven Park

The Grand is a wide river here. Gerard and I have seen it only in its tranquil moods, but in the past, in the spring, its floods caused much damage, especially to bridges. In the winter, though, it showed a very different face. It froze so solidly here that the ice supported winter sports and horse racing, and served as a road for teams and sleighs. Ice was cut and stored for refrigeration.

In the summer the river was the site of water-related amusements and particularly of fishing.

Cayuga was a stop along the canal system, benefiting from the lock at nearby Indiana. Gypsum from Gypsum Mines, a few miles away, was brought by boat to Cayuga where it was transferred to wagons and taken to the railway station. No doubt some of the workers for this and other local industries came from a mostly Irish settlement across the river called Limerick.

Not far from all this bustle, however, was 'a quiet and pleasant rural retreat'—the Hermitage. The house was built by Agnew Patrick Farrell, an Irishman who first settled on the shore of Lake Erie near the mouth of the river and then in 1851 moved to Cayuga. He held several public offices including that of Haldimand's county treasurer, and during the building of the Feeder Canal he was justice of the peace: it was decided that his strong hand (his obituary describes him as 'just to exaction') was the very thing to keep the canal-digging navvies in line.

The Hermitage is a gentleman's residence befitting the son of an Irish landowner. In the 1880s it was described as 'one of the most tasteful dwellings in the County, surrounded by well-kept grounds.'

Other ethnic groups also lived in Cayuga. In the 1850s there were about twenty-five families of escaped slaves from the United States, a reminder that the Underground Railroad led to the north shore of Lake Erie.

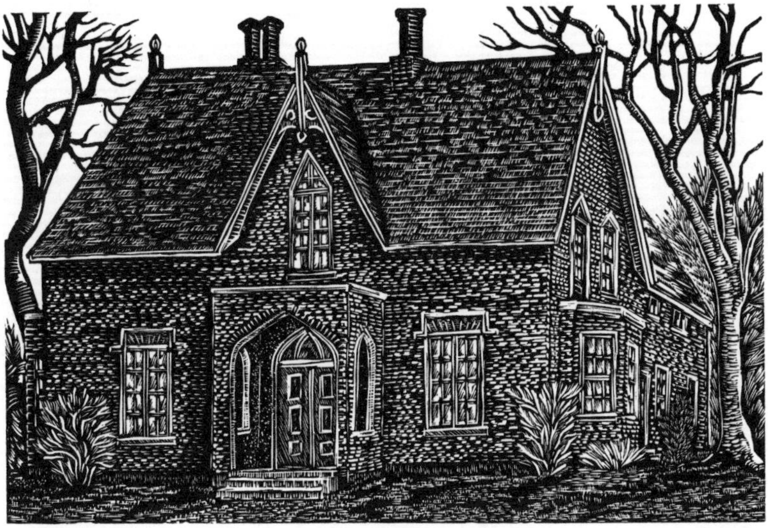

The Hermitage, Cayuga

Between Byng and Dunnville, which are directly across the river from each other, is the dam that channelled water from the Grand River via the Feeder to the Welland Canal. While the dam was being built in 1828–29, and later on during the construction of the canal system, Dunnville must have had the feel of a boom town, with navvies living in shanties and boarding houses and the settlement growing to serve their needs and those of the construction work. Mills and other industries took advantage of the water power created by the dam.

Dunnville's pivotal position continued once the canal system was functioning. Not only did all the shipping pass through it, but goods had to be transshipped from river craft to the vessels taking them through the Feeder to the Welland and beyond. There was a customs house here. The 1850 list of exports from Dunnville to British and foreign ports includes grain, flour, gypsum, timber, and a variety of processed wood products. Boats going upriver carried merchandise for the stores and industries that served the growing numbers of settlers. Like goods, people travelled in both directions. There was at least one shipbuilding firm in the town.

Dunnville is now known for its marshes. The 1877 map shows extensive areas of marsh on either side of the river, including what is now Byng Island Conservation Area on the southwest bank. In early times, these marshes discouraged farming; now they are recognized as an important breeding area for birds and a habitat for fish, and they are used for recreational activities like boating and fishing.

The engraving shows a spot on Sulphur Creek in Byng Island Conservation Area a few yards from where it empties into the river. The scene looks almost tropical with its dense Carolinian forest and sluggish stream, and it is not hard to imagine this life zone stretching from here to the American South.

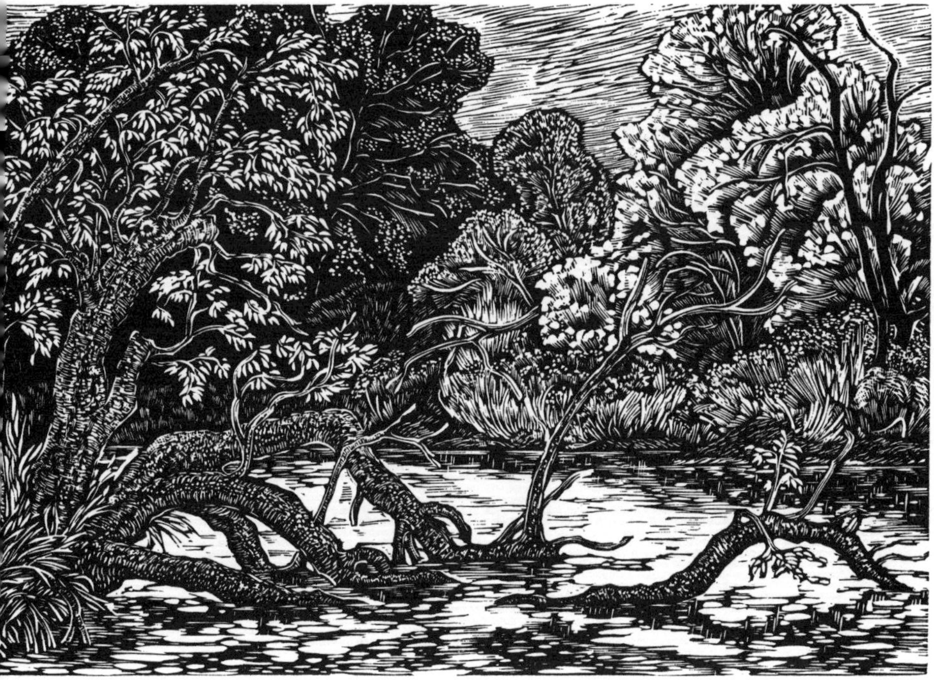

The Grand River at Byng Island

The Port Maitland lock (sometimes incorrectly called Lock 27) is located between Port Maitland and Stromness, just east of the river. It was part of the southwestern extension of the Feeder Canal to Port Maitland and Lake Erie. The building of this second outlet of the Feeder began in about 1842; it is this stretch that, during the time when the southern part of the Second Welland Canal was being built, connected the Feeder and the Welland to Lake Erie.

The lock was also a part of the Grand River canal system because it enabled ships travelling between the river and Lake Erie to bypass the Dunnville dam. Vessels coming downstream entered the Feeder at Dunnville, above the dam, travelled the few miles to Stromness, then turned southwest to follow the extension of the Feeder, going through this lock and rejoining the river at Port Maitland.

The lock, an important historic site, is a fine piece of masonry work. It was built by John L. Brown, a Scottish-born stonemason who also constructed lighthouses and worked on the Erie Canal and on the Second and Third Welland Canals.

As with other sites along the lower part of the river, it requires an effort to imagine the activity that must once have taken place here. The canal has disappeared so the lock is now surrounded by dry land. It was a cold afternoon in November when Gerard and I were here. The sun had set and Gerard was using the very last of the daylight to make his sketch. I stood near the lock listening to the total silence. The land is extremely flat, and the only signs of life were the Port Maitland industries on the horizon. The lock's voice is heard all the more loudly because of the emptiness and stillness of the surrounding area.

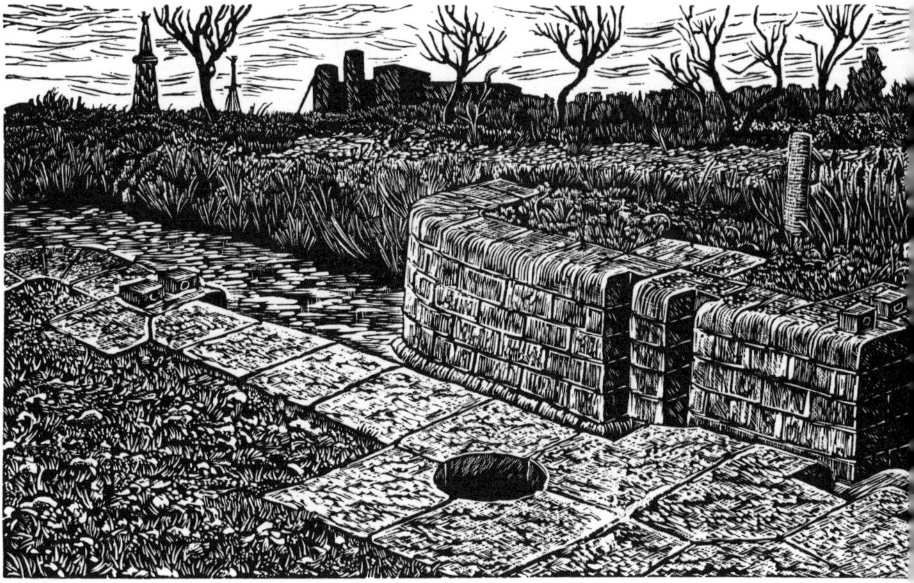

Port Maitland Lock

From this vantage point, on a calm day, we see a peaceful expanse with perhaps a few pleasure boats on it and a freighter on the horizon to remind us that the lake is part of a well-travelled waterway. But someone standing here just after the conclusion of the War of 1812 would have seen possible menace—the danger that hostilities with the U.S. might resume and that across the lake would come enemy ships.

So in 1815 a naval depot was established on the east side of the river, and by the following year it was staffed by a hundred and eighty-seven enlisted men and eight civilians. In 1816 there were four British naval vessels on the lake. The depot consisted of officers' quarters, barracks for other personnel, kitchens, stables, storerooms, and a blacksmith shop. After 1818 this military establishment dwindled gradually, but it stayed at Port Maitland until 1833 when the base for the British Lake Erie naval operations was moved to Port Colborne. However, a village remained.

When the planning for the Welland Canal began in the mid-1820s, Port Maitland was considered as a possible southern terminus because of its harbour, which is large and, in the spring, ice-free several weeks earlier than more easterly ones. During the time when it was the southern outlet of the Welland Canal, a great deal of shipping passed through it.

Port Maitland continues to be a port. It is still home to some of the Lake Erie fishery, and it is and has been the site of industries engaged in chemicals manufacturing and ship recycling. It is also a harbour for pleasure boats.

The lighthouse on the pier reminds us of the town's past and present identity as a harbour and as the centre of a spider's web of industry and transportation.

And, looking out over the lake, we realize that, from here, the water of the river flows out into the larger world.

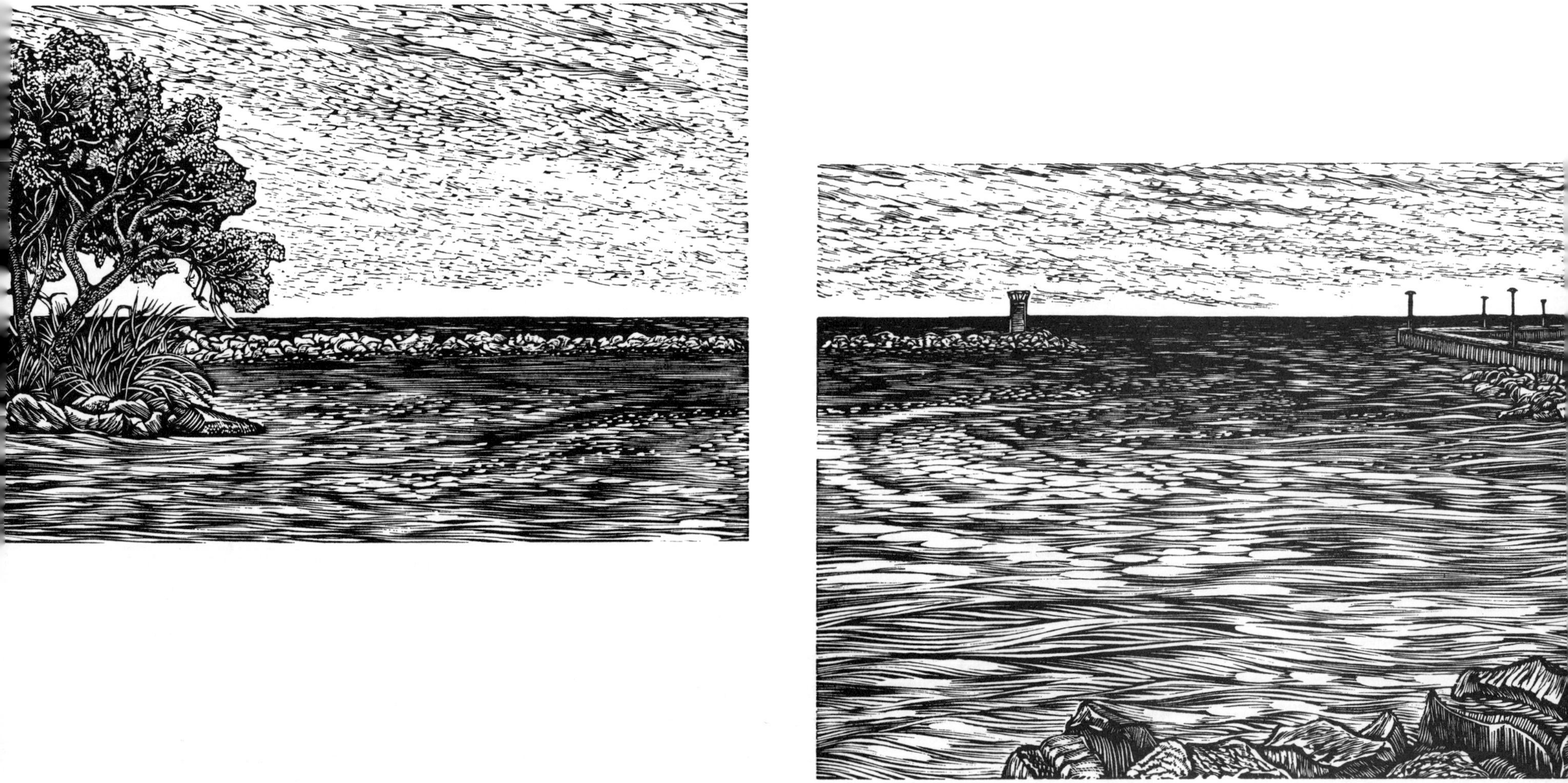

The Mouth of the Grand River, Port Maitland

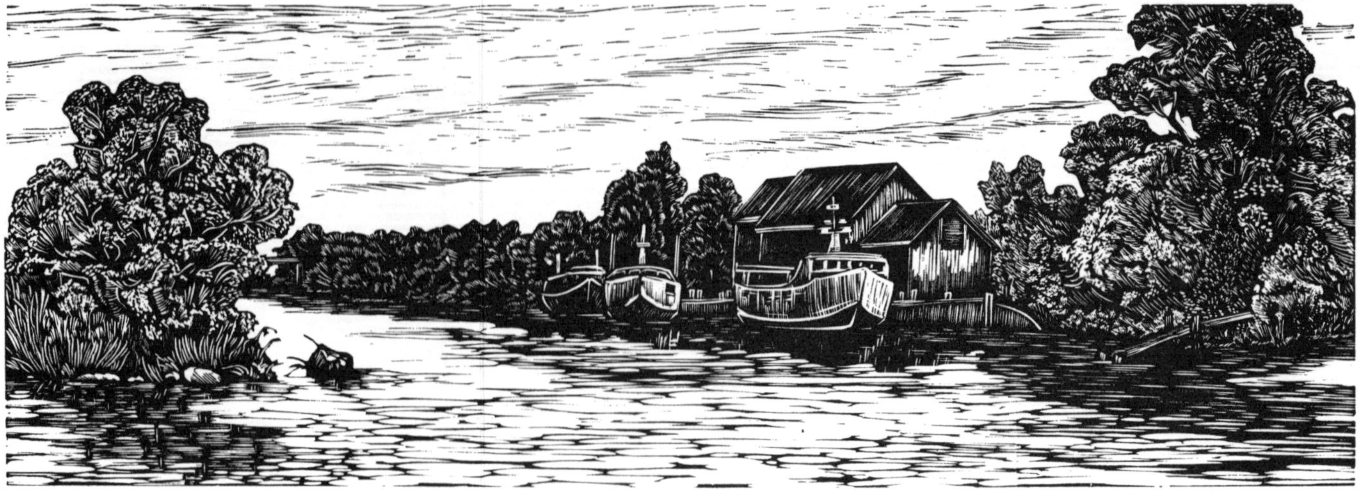

Fishing Boats at Port Maitland

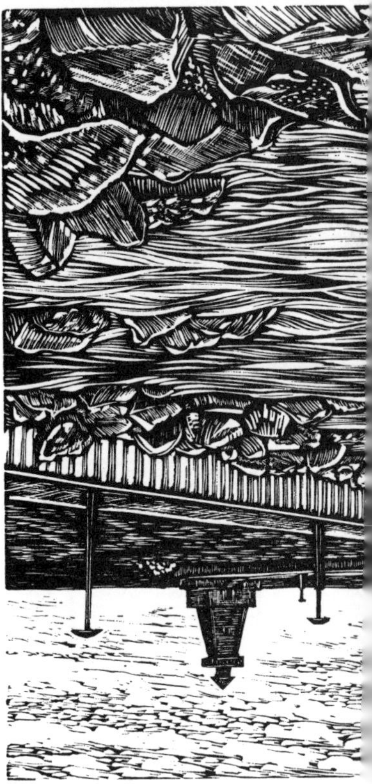

This image is a fitting conclusion to the series, because it clearly illustrates the interaction of the Grand River, the Feeder Canal, and Lake Erie. These fishing boats are moored along the banks of the Feeder, just yards from the left bank of the river, and are used for fishing in the lake. They are also a link with history: people have been fishing here since the retreating glaciers left in their wake the body of water that is now Lake Erie. The commercial fishery began in the 1820s.

Port Maitland was once a busy fishing port; in the first half of the twentieth century more than fifty fish tugs and fishing boats operated from here, and boats from Dunnville would have passed through the Port Maitland harbour as well.

Lake Erie is still one of the biggest freshwater fisheries in the world, even though the earlier species—whitefish, blue pike, herring, and trout—are gone, destroyed by overfishing, pollution, and the invasion of the sea lamprey. The lake now contains an abundance of smelt (originally an invader from the Atlantic) but there are insufficient markets for it.

Water quality and related issues connect the river and the lake. Pollution from the river enters the lake; invasive fish species from the lake find their way upriver. In the 1970s, the lake was so seriously polluted by nutrients that it was considered to be on the verge of death, but since then there has been a considerable improvement, both in the quality of the water and in the fish species inhabiting it.

Water quality is one of the elements that most firmly connects the story of the whole Grand River watershed from the river's many sources to its mouth—as it does in the case of every river on the planet. Everything that happens upriver in some way affects what happens downriver, and the whole watershed of about 6,800 square kilometres funnels down to this spot.

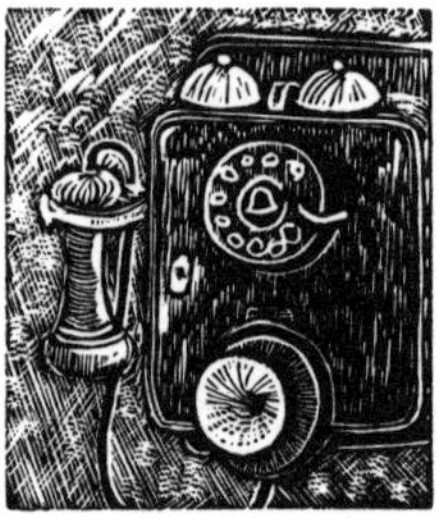

— *Echoes and Connections* —

At the beginning of the introduction I drew a word-picture of Gerard sketching by the river. The images in this book derive from the wood engravings based on those sketches and are reproduced here in the engravings' original size.

Though Gerard and I don't live in the Grand River valley (we're one watershed to the west), we've 'lived with' the Grand for many years. We made nearly two dozen trips to it between 2004 and 2008 and another dozen-plus in 2012–13. In each trip we focused on a short section, looking for scenes to sketch, buildings and objects to research. Later trips were illuminated by the research done in the interval since earlier ones. The first series led to Gerard's creation of a handmade, limited-edition book titled *A Pebble's Journey: The Grand River Observed by Two Artists*—his images, my text—which Gerard published in the spring of 2010.

From sketch to finished wood engraving is in itself a journey. The sketch is used as the basis for a detailed drawing, which is then transferred to tracing paper and, after being reversed, is redrawn onto a block of (preferably) boxwood. Then, using fine and very sharp chisel-like gravers called burins, Gerard engraves the image into the hard surface of the wood, making it three-dimensional.

The wood-engraving process that created the images in this book is therefore parallel, in miniature, to the way in which the river engraves the landscape. The small reflects the large.

And the specific points to the general. By its nature, this book is a series of still images. But they are stills from a large, complex, and multi-layered film.

Such echoes also characterize the watershed as a whole. Small local issues can have implications that go far beyond themselves. For instance, the Grand River Conservation Authority and its partners and many volunteers have restored Mill Creek, whose water enters the Grand just north of Cayuga. In the 1960s, the GRCA had built a dam on the creek to create a thirty-seven-hectare reservoir in the Taquanyah Conservation Area for irrigation and recreation. But the reservoir damaged aquatic life, partly because it turned a cold-water stream into a warm-water one, thus driving out many desirable fish species that prefer cold water. So in 2004–5 the dam was removed, and the moonscape left by the draining of the reservoir was rehabilitated. Since then, more than 10,000 shrubs and trees typical of the Carolinian zone have been planted, and ponds and wetlands have been created. Mill Creek is now once again a cold-water stream, and the water that it delivers into the Grand helps to cool the water downriver. The restored Carolinian ecosystem in Taquanyah is habitat for wildlife and makes the Carolinian zone that much less threatened. Socially speaking, the process of restoring the ecosystem has connected many local people with ecological and environmental issues.

These interactions and implications help to make the complexity of a watershed more understandable, and the story of the Grand—and of many other rivers—is full of them.

One of the aspects of the Grand River's 'riverness' is its function as a living laboratory: you can almost hear the dialogue between the people who had an impact on the river in the past, and the river's replies, and the responses of those living with and managing the river now. Back and forth the dialogue goes, with contributions from all the components of the ecosystem. Learning to understand this conversation is a major task for today's river managers and scientists, and it has implications for planet-wide water issues because, again, all rivers behave in much the same way. What works in one place is at least worth trying somewhere else. The GRCA's work was recognized in 2000 when it received the International River*prize*, awarded for fifty years of successful restoration work on a much-damaged river.

In other ways as well, the Grand River's importance goes far beyond the immediate watershed. In 1994, the Canadian Heritage Rivers System, an organization that promotes, protects, and enhances Canada's river heritage, designated the Grand as a Heritage River. It was the first time that a whole watershed was chosen; until then, only portions of rivers had been designated. Moreover, the Grand was the first river in the more settled part of the country to be honoured; all the others up to that time were wilderness rivers, or rivers in protected areas such as national parks. The designation of the Grand recognizes the natural heritage of the region, such as Luther Marsh and the Carolinian forest, the recreational opportunities, and the human heritage. The latter includes the watershed's cultural mosaic, the thousands of years of occupation by First Peoples, the industrial history, and the many significant historic sites.

This heritage designation has involved more than just a plaque. To receive it, the GRCA had to produce a detailed management plan for the preservation and restoration of the watershed and the promotion of its health. Because the Grand is in the more densely settled part of Canada, river management here is complex. It is shared among all levels of government, the First Peoples, and many non-governmental organizations. The management plan—titled *The Grand Strategy for Managing the Grand River as a Canadian Heritage River*—was the result of extensive public participation.

As noted above, this book is our second run at the subject of the Grand River. *A Pebble's Journey* contained forty engravings, together with my brief introduction and conclusion and, accompanying each engraving, a caption of a few sentences in length. Even as we were creating that book we knew that there was a great deal more that we could have shown and written about the river, and the plan to produce something like the present one was constantly in our minds. Some parts of that earlier publication—a number of the engravings, and fragments of text—are incorporated in this present one. However, many of the images are new and so is most of the text, the result of further research and of many more trips to the river.

Throughout the process, the two of us reflected on and discussed riverness, the life and character and actions of rivers, a watershed as an organizing unit of landscape just as municipalities are administrative units of society. We were fascinated by what we observed about the way water moves and how it relates to stream banks, boulders, vegetation, and human-built structures like bridges and mills. We explored and discussed many aspects of the area's history. In the earlier book we stayed very close to the river's banks, but in the present one we have allowed ourselves somewhat more latitude, while still showing how everything is connected with the river. Those discussions are reflected in our choice of subjects and our approach to them, in the design of the images, and in my text.

It is probably because my field is words that I keep returning in my mind to the idea that when we stand by the Grand River we are hearing and seeing its timeless dialogue with soil, rock, vegetation, weather, humans and—because moving water is pulled by gravity—with the planet itself.

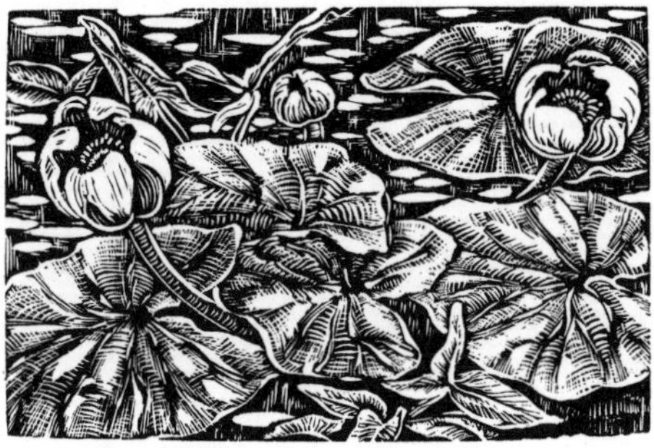

— *Further Reading* —

Abley, Mark, *Conversations with a Dead Man: The Legacy of Duncan Campbell Scott.* Madeira Park, BC: Douglas & McIntyre (2013) Ltd., 2013.

Chapple, Nina Perkins, *A Heritage of Stone: Buildings of the Niagara Peninsula, Fergus and Elora, Guelph, Region of Waterloo, Cambridge, Paris, Ancaster-Dundas-Flamborough, Hamilton and St. Marys.* Toronto: James Lorimer & Co., Ltd., 2006.

De Visser, John, and the Grand Valley Conservation Foundation, *Grand River Reflections.* Erin, Boston Mills Press, 1989.

Dunham, Mabel, *Grand River.* Toronto: McClelland and Stewart, 1945.

Fischer, George, and Mark Harris, *Ontario's Historic Mills.* Erin: Boston Mills Press, 2007.

Gray, Charlotte, *Flint & Feather: The Life and Times of E. Pauline Johnson, Tekahionwake.* Toronto: HarperCollins Publishers Ltd., 2002.

Hewitt, Kenneth, *Elora Gorge: A Visitor's Guide.* Toronto: Stoddart Publishing Co. Ltd., 1995.

Johnson, Lorraine, *The Natural Treasures of Carolinian Canada: Discovering the Rich Natural Diversity of Ontario's Southwestern Heartland.* Toronto: James Lorimer & Co., 2007.

Miller, Muriel, *Homer Watson: The Man of Doon.* Toronto: Summerhill Press, 1988.

Nelson, Gordon, and others, *Towards a* Grand *Sense of Place: Writings on changing environments, land-uses, landscapes, lifestyles and planning of a Canadian Heritage River.* Waterloo, ON: Heritage Resources Centre, University of Waterloo, 2004.

Paxton, James W., *Joseph Brant and His World.* Toronto: James Lorimer & Co., 2008.

Rogers, Edward S., and Donald B. Smith, *Aboriginal Ontario: Historical Perspectives on the First Nations.* Toronto: Dundurn Press, 1994.

Smardz Frost, Karolyn, and others, *Ontario's African-Canadian Heritage: Collected Writings by Fred Landon, 1918–1967*. Toronto: Natural Heritage Books, 2009.

Smith, Donald B., *Sacred Feathers: The Reverend Peter Jones (Kahkewaquonaby) and the Mississauga Indians*. Toronto: University of Toronto Press, 1987.

Styran, Roberta M., and Robert R. Taylor, *Mr. Merritt's Ditch: A Welland Canals Album*. Toronto: Stoddart Publishing Co. Ltd., 1992.

For notes and a comprehensive list of sources please see http://www.mariannebrandis.ca.

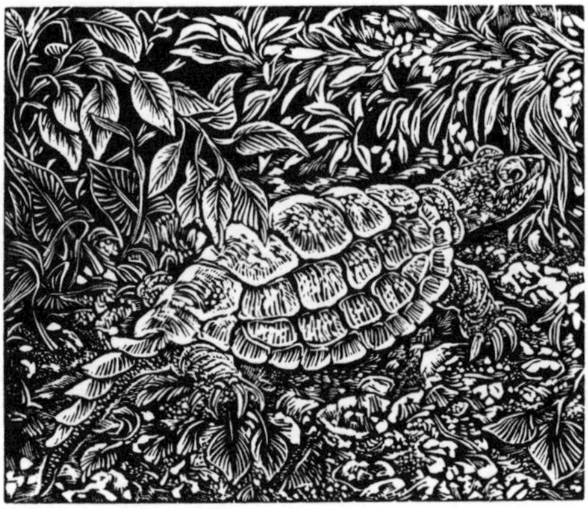

— Acknowledgements —

We would like to thank Tim and Elke Inkster for their usual superb book design and for their help and supportiveness when an injury to Marianne's right hand interfered with her work on later stages of preparing the manuscript. We would also like to thank Chandra Wohleber for her astute and sympathetic editing.

There are many people whom we wish to thank for various kinds of help: Rob Adlam, Jennifer Asimoudis, Beth Dempster, Robert Gaede, Mary Gartshore, John Kneale, Barbara Martindale, Scott McKowen, Rych Mills, Homer Moelchert, Bradley Marlen Moggach, Alan Morgan, Mary V. Nelles, Pat Nelles, Ken Parker, Fred A. Michah Rynor, Sybil B. Rynor, Robert Shipley, Marg Smith, Janet Straker, Donald and Louise Stroh, Roberta M. Styran, Janette Veal, William Warnick, Gary Warrick, and Robert Woolner.

Our hosts, guides, and informants at historic sites and other organizations were—in person or by phone or e-mail—extremely helpful:

Brian Wood at the Bell Homestead National Historic Site; Bradley Melle at the Chiefswood National Historic Site; Lynn Griggs and Dan Schmalz at the City of Cambridge Archives; Wayne Townsend at the Dufferin County Museum and Archives; Mardi Tindal at Five Oaks Education and Retreat Centre of The United Church of Canada; Connie J. Stubbs at Georgia-Pacific Canada, Inc.; Ralph Beaumont, Dave Schultz, and Gregg Zwiers at the Grand River Conservation Authority; Karen Richardson at the Haldimand County Museum and Archives; Susan Burke at Joseph Schneider Haus in Kitchener; Karen Ball-Pyatt and Kate Hagerman at the Kitchener Public Library; Kevin Reid at the Ontario Commercial Fisheries Association; Lindsay Benjamin at the Region of Waterloo; Betty Mitchell at the former Dochstader Hotel; Elysia DeLaurentis and Kimberley Somerville at the Wellington County Museum and Archives; and Paula Whitlow at the Woodland

Cultural Centre. We also received valuable help from the staff at Ruthven Park National Historic Site, the Stratford-Perth Archives, and the Waterloo Region Museum. The owner of the former Middleport general store kindly showed us around and gave us useful information.

Our warm thanks to Helen Brink for information to quote the passage on page 74.

In the end, we wish to note that any mistakes are ours.

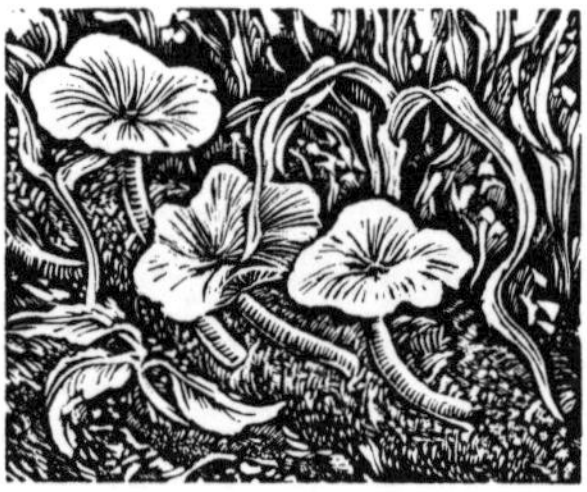

— *About the Artist* —

A member of the Wood Engravers' Network, Gerard Brender à Brandis has produced hundreds of drawings, wood engravings, and watercolours of plants, landscape, buildings, and musical instruments. These images have appeared in books, including *Wood, Ink and Paper, A Wood Engraver's Alphabet*, and *Concord of Sweet Sounds* (all published by the Porcupine's Quill), as well as in his own handmade editions. His work is represented in the collections of the Royal Botanical Gardens (Hamilton, Ontario), the Missouri Botanic Garden, the Arnold Arboretum, the Hunt Botanical Library, and many others. His garden and his studio are located in Stratford, Ontario.

— *About the Author* —

Marianne Brandis came to Canada from the Netherlands in 1947. After earning her BA and MA from McMaster University, she worked in radio and taught at Ryerson Polytechnical Institute (now University) before becoming a full-time writer. Most of her work has a historical element. She is the author of award-winning historical fiction and has also written biography and memoirs. Pursuing her interest in the relations between people and their surroundings, she has researched and written about Toronto's ravines, environmental and social issues in Malawi, and urban design and planning projects in her current hometown of Stratford, Ontario.